Unmasking the Entrepreneur

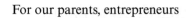

For our parents, entrepreneurs

Unmasking the Entrepreneur

Campbell Jones

University of Leicester School of Management, UK

André Spicer

Warwick Business School, University of Warwick, UK

Edward Elgar
Cheltenham, UK • Northampton, MA, USA

Published by
Edward Elgar Publishing Limited
The Lypiatts
15 Lansdown Road
Cheltenham
Glos GL50 2JA
UK

Edward Elgar Publishing, Inc.
William Pratt House
9 Dewey Court
Northampton
Massachusetts 01060
USA

A catalogue record for this book
is available from the British Library

Library of Congress Control Number: 2009936381

Mixed Sources
Product group from well-managed
forests and other controlled sources
www.fsc.org Cert no. SA-COC-1565
© 1996 Forest Stewardship Council
FSC

ISBN 978 1 84542 654 5 (cased)
      978 1 84844 844 5 (paperback)

Printed and bound by MPG Books Group, UK

Contents

Acknowledgements

This book is the product of more than ten years of frequently interrupted work. Over this time, the ideas in this book have benefited from often brutal feedback and debate. This has occurred at seminars at Copenhagen Business School, the University of Stockholm, Swinburne University of Technology, the University of Lancaster, the University of Leicester, the University of the West of England, Växjö University and Victoria University Wellington. We also benefited from feedback on papers we presented at ESRC seminars at the University of Liverpool and the Open University.

Ideas in this book have also been presented at a number of conferences, of which we can recall the Association of Social Anthropologists of Aotearoa/ New Zealand in Dunedin (1998), the Critical Management Studies Conference in Manchester (2001), the Colloquium on Text and Economics in Antwerp (2002), the Organizational Discourse conference in Amsterdam (2004), the Movements in Entrepreneurship Research conference in Reykjavik (2005), the Standing Conference for Organizational Symbolism in Stockholm (2005), the European Group for Organization Studies conference in Bergen (2006), the Standing Conference for Organizational Symbolism in Nijmegen (2006), the Theorizing Entrepreneurship workshop in Leicester (2006) and the Academy of Management Congress in Atlanta (2006). We would like to thank participants in all of these fora for their comments.

Earlier versions of several chapters of this book have been published previously, and appear here extensively revised, and with some of their interconnections hopefully made more clear. We thank the following publishers for permission to rework material that previously appeared as:

Jones, C. and A. Spicer (2005) 'The sublime object of entrepreneurship', *Organization*, 12(2): 223–46.

Jones, C. and A. Spicer (2005) 'Outline of a genealogy of the value of the entrepreneur' in G. Erreygers and G. Jacobs (eds), *Language, Communication and the Economy*. Amsterdam: Benjamins.

Jones, C. and A. Spicer (2006) 'Entrepreneurial excess' in J. Brewis, S. Linstead, D. Boje and T. O'Shea (eds), *The Passion of Organizing*. Copenhagen: Abstrakt.

Jones, C. and A. Spicer (2009) 'Is the Marquis de Sade an entrepreneur?' in D. Hjorth and C. Steyaert (eds), *The Politics and Aesthetics of Entrepreneurship*. Cheltenham, UK and Northampton, MA, USA: Edward Elgar.

Every effort has been made to trace all the copyright holders but if any have been inadvertently overlooked, the publishers will be pleased to make the necessary arrangements at the first opportunity.

This book has been influenced directly and indirectly by a number of colleagues, both through direct feedback and by our reading their work. This will be seen throughout the book. We thank all of those who have been involved, and in particular would like to thank Paul du Gay, Peter Fleming, Shayne Grice, Daniel Hjorth, Anna-Maria Murtola, Alf Rehn, Bent Meier Sørensen and Chris Steyaert. We also thank Daniel Hjorth, Anna-Maria Murtola and Lena Olaison, who read the complete manuscript and made many very useful suggestions for improvements. Ultimately, of course, we are responsible for the many shortcomings that still remain.

We dedicate this book to our parents, Jenni and Allan Jones and Alan and Berris Spicer. They have been involved in entrepreneurial ventures throughout their lives. Through their work and their lives they have taught us about entrepreneurship as creating something with and for others.

1. 'I am an entrepreneur'

In a photograph taken on the street of a large US city, we find an African American man sitting on the sidewalk, looking at pedestrians passing by. He huddles under a blanket of some kind. Any passer-by instantly recognises this essential character in the drama of American city life. He is the homeless person, the bum, the rough sleeper, the vagrant, the pan-handler, the vagabond. And naturally the passer-by does not want to look too closely. They are scared that this street dweller might catch their eye and ask whether they might spare a brother a dime. But if the fleet-footed city stroller happened to stop and look, just for one second, they might notice something. The sign he holds does not proclaim the usual narratives which identify this man as a victim ('have AIDS', 'have no money', 'lost job'), or as a street-side Dionysian ('want money for beer'). The sign explicitly states 'I am no beggar'. The sign tells us that he is an 'entrepreneur' who offers you a service of cleaning your car windows.

There are many more attractive images of the entrepreneur, of course. But as we prepared this book we found all these appealing and heroic allusions somewhat unsatisfying. They did not capture the darker side of the entrepreneur and entrepreneurship (Kets de Vries, 1985). They did not seem to register that the reality of entrepreneurship is not massive success but one of struggle, stress, debt and failure. This pushed us to discard the celebratory ways of thinking about the entrepreneur and consider some more dismal ones: the bankrupt, the petty criminal, the swindler, the oppressed factory worker. But one image stuck in our minds, and we came back to it again and again. A beggar with a sign claiming to be an entrepreneur.

For us, this image captures much of what the study of entrepreneurship has missed. At the most basic level, it reminds us that entrepreneurship is not an easy ride. The reality is that most entrepreneurs' lives are not filled with success and private jets. Rather, they involve more often than not business failures. Indeed, many would-be entrepreneurs often end up precisely where our unlikely entrepreneur is – on the street. The image also reminds us that entrepreneurship today can be almost anything. We notice this homeless person making an appeal to notions of entrepreneurialism. By doing so, he is using the term to cast a positive light on a set of activities we usually think about negatively. This reminds us that not only does everyone claim to be an entrepreneur these days, but that being an entrepreneur is always presented as a good thing. By appealing to the label, our 'unlikely entrepreneur' is able to cast off the negative associations of his occupation of window washing and try to cast himself in a more positive light. Finally, this image reminds us that despite the fact that the term entrepreneur can mean almost anything and everything, there are in fact certain limits about who can successfully claim the mantle. The person seeing this unfortunate character on the street might laugh to themselves – they might think: of course this individual is not an entrepreneur. How could he be! Entrepreneurs are successful characters who are dressed to kill. The viewer may think – after all, the person we have before us clearly has no income, no prospects – how could they consider themselves to be an entrepreneur! This mismatch between the statement ('I am an entrepreneur') and the reality (but actually I am a homeless man who is desperately hungry) shows us that despite the myths, the identity of being an entrepreneur is not available to everyone. Rather, it is a limited title, only conferred upon the successful few who actually manage to make it. In many ways, the field of entrepreneurship *is* this shocking difference between the overblown rhetoric and horrible reality.

This disturbing image of entrepreneurship prompted us to recognise that while there might have been many celebrations and some cold descriptions and analyses of entrepreneurship, there have been a few – but as we will argue, nowhere near enough – critical accounts of entrepreneurship. This is one of the central aims of this book: we want to develop and extend the critical theory of entrepreneurship. From the outset, we should stress that this does not involve a complete rejection of entrepreneurship, and hence this book is not 'against entrepreneurship'. We think that there is much that is positive and progressive in notions such as innovation, creativity and freedom of expression. These are things that we will seek to defend, and in this sense we are in favour of them to the extent that they represent entrepreneurship. Our problem, however, is that although these things are often appealed to in order to shore up the merits of entrepreneurship, they are far too often merely rhetorical appeals behind which something more sinister lurks.

One of the key paradoxes of entrepreneurship research then – and one that we will animate us throughout this book – is that thinking about entrepreneurship has been remarkably lacking in creativity or innovation. Entrepreneurship has become a mantra that has worked, paradoxically, by repetition of the same. Business gurus repeat the same platitudes about the virtues of enterprise. These are echoed by politicians seeking economic cures. And academic researchers have bureaucratised entrepreneurship research into a mundane game of collecting statistics and operationalising every variable that might in any way be related to entrepreneurship. Where is innovation when it comes to the concept of entrepreneurship itself?

In this book we argue against the figure of the entrepreneur that prevails in much of business practice and in popular and academic representations of the entrepreneur. To put it as bluntly as we can, we argue that this talk about entrepreneurship is, more often than not, a shiny veneer behind which there is much that is troubling. We will argue that almost all of the intellectual efforts – both by academics and by practitioners of entrepreneurship – have rested on shabby grounds, unthought premises, weak argumentation and scant evidence. We will try to demonstrate how these conceptual and political problems with entrepreneurship work, and how they are interconnected.

In this sense, far from being opposed to creativity, one might think of this book as an effort to make entrepreneurship research more entrepreneurial. As Chris Steyaert and Daniel Hjorth (2003) have insisted, there is a pressing need to make entrepreneurship more welcoming to the creativity, innovation and joyfulness that it purports to support. Of course, to do something like this will involve what Joseph Schumpeter (1934) famously called 'creative destruction'. In the same way that he spoke of the way that entrepreneurs who were to create something anew had to destroy previous combinations of resources, in this book we too will engage in a similar effort to take apart some of the fundamental combinations on which entrepreneurship stands. The point here should be clear. If entrepreneurship research is to be taken seriously then it needs to be willing to take risks. It will need to be open to the new, in fact it must welcome novelty and change, which means that many of the cherished ways of proceeding that have now solidified as the common sense of entrepreneurship will have to be cleared away. We propose, then, nothing less than to *unmask entrepreneurship*.

UNMASKING?

What do we mean when we speak of 'unmasking'? Do we mean that entrepreneurship is a falsehood, under which the truth lies concealed? Are we suggesting that we have been to the mountain and are now returning with the truth for all to behold? Some might think that to speak of unmasking, we are using a rather outdated or simple-minded idea of truth. One might ask if truth is really out there waiting to be discovered and then delivered as if on tablets from a mountain. Many social scientists today are critical of the idea that truth is such a simple matter of revelation. Truth, they tell us, is not so much a matter of revelation as of negotiation. Truth is socially constructed and contested, and cannot simply be read off from the nature of the world.

While we accept much of this, we will insist throughout this book on speaking of unmasking. We do not think that any way of reading the world is as good as any other, or that the consequences of different readings are morally equivalent. But more so, we think that many otherwise well-meaning liberal academics have retreated from taking responsibility for the claims that continue to circulate in public life. There remains a task for social and intellectual criticism, and although we need to be aware of the implausibility of simplistic ideas of truth, we should not use this as an excuse for failing to be clear about our positions and to give reasons for why we hold them.

When we use the word 'unmasking' here, we are evoking the distinction that Martin Heidegger (2002) made between two concepts of truth. Heidegger has argued that the Ancient Greeks had two quite distinct concepts of truth, even if today we only recognise one of these. The first, which is still in currency today, is the idea of truth as 'correctness'. On this view, truth is a matter of approximation or rightness, and something will be true if it matches up with the world or with a set of conventions governing the production of true statements. But the Greeks also had another concept of truth, which we have all but forgotten today. This is the idea of truth as 'unconcealing'. Following this idea, the task of thinking is not to find a pre-existing truth, but rather a matter of struggling to move away from the particular ways in which we happen to be blinded at a particular moment. Truth as unconcealing is not a matter of accuracy but rather a matter of invention. It is not a matter of discovery but a matter of production.

When in this book we speak of 'unmasking' then, it can be thought of in a similar way. We are not going to assert that we have discovered the truth of entrepreneurship, and we certainly do not have any sense that our work on entrepreneurship is anything like definitive. But we might suggest that we have, drawing on the ideas of many other thinkers who have come before us, assembled these ideas in a unique combination so as to shed new light on entrepreneurship. This does not mean that we will, in a puff of smoke, reveal entrepreneurship in all its mysteries. But it does mean that we will show how entrepreneurship can be thought of in very different ways than it often is, and that these different ways might be important.

That being said, our efforts at unmasking will also at times rest on a notion of truth as correctness. But we think that entrepreneurship researchers have far too often assumed this conception of truth, and have tried to mirror entrepreneurship in its truth. We propose here a different project, which is a work of creative destruction that will unconceal entrepreneurship in particular ways. Even if we only find a second mask behind the first mask, and behind that yet another, this is for us not a reason to stop seeking to unmask – which would mean to stop thinking – but rather is the reason for more efforts to follow on from our efforts in this short book.

THE TASK OF THINKING

Throughout this book we draw on writings in philosophy and critical social theory in order to unmask the entrepreneur. We have found it especially productive to think about this task of thinking in the terms outlined by Gilles Deleuze and Félix Guattari in their book *What is Philosophy?* In this book, they make the case for a particularly productive conception of philosophy as the domain of human activity involved in the creation of concepts. They build on the earlier work of Friedrich Nietzsche, who argues that we should not 'accept concepts as gifts', but 'should *make* and *create* them' (Nietzsche, 1968: 220). For Deleuze and Guattari 'Philosophy is the art of forming, inventing, and fabricating concepts' (Deleuze and Guattari, 1994: 2). Indeed, the whole history of philosophy can be read as the successive creation of concepts. What we are seeking to do here is to create new concepts with which we can think about the entrepreneur. The second thing which Deleuze and Guattari argue that philosophy should do is to clarify the grounds on which a concept rests. This involves tracing out the philosophical and theoretical landscape in which a figure like the entrepreneur dwells. It involves showing how a concept is linked with a whole series of pre-philosophical assumptions in which it is grounded. For us, unmasking the entrepreneur involves teasing out the pre-philosophical assumptions upon which this concept rests. Therefore, this is a philosophical book in the sense that we are seeking to clarify the concept of entrepreneurship and to create a new concept of what entrepreneurship might be.

Having said this, we should add two caveats. First, concepts always exist in relation to earlier concepts. In this book we have sought to draw freely on concepts from a very wide range of thinkers. As you will see, this book is peopled with many theorists from the past, and we will apologise in advance to readers who are baffled by our choice of thinkers and the combinations in which we arrange them. We can only note that this is a self-conscious effort on our part to avoid, as much as is possible, the kind of dogmatism that can set in if we were forced to occupy something like a stable 'position' or 'perspective', and with this an agreed body of theory to draw on, before we could say anything. In this respect we are perhaps departing from the way that theory has often been done by academics who are more interested in disciplinary propriety. We are of course, far from the first to draw on eclectic sources in order to identify diverse aspects of a phenomenon. As you will note, our unmasking will require that we as authors put on several masks ourselves, and that we are willing and able to take these off so as to approach our object from a different angle later.

A second caveat relating to theory is that we have no interest here in being abstract for the sake of abstraction. Many see theory as something that takes us away from the earth. It is criticised for being 'just theory', disengaged from reality and from events in the world. Let us be clear that we also are very aware of this danger, and have no interest in abstraction as such. In fact, one of our major objections to 'talk' about entrepreneurship is that it is far too often extremely abstract. In particular academic entrepreneurship research has displayed a remarkable tendency towards the abstract, in the sense of model building and assertions in the absence of – or directly in conflict with – the actual realities of economic life. If anything, our theoretical and philosophical unmasking of entrepreneurship will attempt to dismantle some of the abstractions of entrepreneurship researchers. This will not just be done in the name of a blunt 'concrete world' that will automatically interrupt the abstractions of entrepreneurship. Rather, it will involve a theoretical journey *through* abstraction that keeps an eye keenly on the dangers of theoreticism.

THIS BOOK

In the next chapter we look at what existing studies have said about entrepreneurship, and what a critical approach to entrepreneurship might involve. We begin by dividing existing theories of entrepreneurship into three major camps. The first involves functionalist approaches, which seek to identify what causes entrepreneurship and the outcomes associated with entrepreneurship. The second are interpretive approaches, which tend to focus on how entrepreneurship is conducted on a day-to-day level. We argue that while both of these provide important insights, they are crucially lacking in a number of ways. For these reasons we identify a third approach to entrepreneurship – a critical approach. This critical approach broadly seeks to question the category of the entrepreneur. It does so by focusing on the politics associated with the category of entrepreneurship, and asks who can and cannot count as an entrepreneur, and what is involved representing someone as such. It involves asking what is at stake when we call someone an entrepreneur, and the way that entrepreneurship is used to further embed power relations. Building on recent studies, we identify a number of core characteristics of a critique of entrepreneurship. These are a critique of representations of the entrepreneur, a critique of affects associated with the entrepreneur, a critique of the structural limitations, and a critique of agency which points out the way in which the category of the entrepreneur is actively and creatively used and negotiated.

In Chapter 3 we focus on some representations of entrepreneurship found in various studies of entrepreneurship as well as in popular discourse. We show the way that discourse around entrepreneurship is highly ambiguous, and tends to involve a repeated 'failure'. This is evident in the fact that repeated attempts to identify what is specific about the entrepreneur have failed, and entrepreneurship discourse circles around this 'gap' or 'lack'. This lack does not make notions of entrepreneurship less attractive, but actually makes them more attractive and engaging. This leads us to argue that the entrepreneur should be conceived as a 'sublime object', that is, a figure of discourse which is attractive but ultimately empty. It is this emptiness that makes the discourse of the entrepreneur so desirable.

Chapter 4 outlines a genealogy of representations of the entrepreneur. Scrutinising texts from the early physiocrats through to Schumpeter and beyond, we examine how the entrepreneur has gradually emerged as a figure within economic thought. We also look at the changing face of the entrepreneur in its transition from being seen as an adventurous trader to an innovator and even a corporate manager. We show that what is particularly interesting about this history is the fact that slowly the entrepreneur came to be understood as a source of value in its own right. This means that by making a claim that one is entrepreneurial, it is then possible to claim an increased share of the proceeds of production. Doing this masks many of the other claims to value that might legitimately be made.

In Chapter 5, we account for the expenditure of claimed value. We argue that the central issue with entrepreneurs is not that they are cold, calculating characters. Rather they often display a measure of irrational exuberance. The entrepreneur is not just a character who produces, but also a figure who is given the role of excessive consumption and waste. The entrepreneur benefits from a special role in being able to lay claim to wasting resources – whether from excessive individual displays of entrepreneurial vigour, minor individual attempts to be entrepreneurial, or massive government investment in programmes designed to encourage entrepreneurship.

In Chapters 6 and 7, we look at two further cases of unlikely entrepreneurs. In particular, we ask why, if the idea of entrepreneurship is so general, cannot everyone be counted as an entrepreneur? In order to explore this question, Chapter 6 takes up the 'extreme case' of the infamous Marquis de Sade. If we look at Sade's proposals and propositions we notice that he engages in many acts that should properly be considered as 'institutional entrepreneurship'. Nevertheless, we note that Sade is unrecognisable as an entrepreneur in the dominant code of entrepreneurship discourse because he offends a range of deeply held moral codes. This makes it clear that one of the central limitations of whether someone can be considered an entrepreneur or not is bound up with a whole set of moral evaluations.

In the following chapter, we continue to ask who cannot lay claim to being an entrepreneur. We take up another figure who engages in significant entrepreneurial activity, but is typically not considered to be an entrepreneur: the illegal immigrant. Building on a burgeoning range of studies that look at the grey economy, we examine a case which brought about major debate about the role of illegal immigrants in the English economy. This was the drowning of 23 illegal immigrants collecting cockles in Morecambe Bay in 2004. We note that these immigrants, although undertaking what should probably be coded as entrepreneurial activities, were not seen as entrepreneurs. Instead they were represented as a range of other types (from family members to aspirational workers). We argue that the reason that they were not understood as being entrepreneurs was the fact that they were operating illegally. This highlights a second aspect of what is involved in entrepreneurialism, namely, the place of law and the state in questions of entrepreneurship. We thus emphasise the way that the state identifies something as being either legal or illegal. We suggest that instead of being considered to be something opposing entrepreneurship, the state is actually foundational in proscribing and constructing the possibility for what is enterprising and what is not.

In Chapter 8, we take these arguments regarding the ethical and legal dimension further. We do this by pointing out that entrepreneurship must have an ethical dimension to function effectively, and we clarify the meaning of the ethical. Building on existing debates about the ethics of entrepreneurship, we seek to clarify the basis on which something might be considered to be good or bad entrepreneurialism. We notice that the few existing studies that outline a sustained normative position on the entrepreneur tend to rely upon latent and undefended assumptions about individualism. Questioning these assumptions, we argue that an ethical consideration of the entrepreneur needs to be premised not upon an ethic of the isolated individual, but rather, it needs to recognise that entrepreneurship always involves working with others. In particular, it involves an attempt to create the capacity of the other to innovate rather than claiming innovation for one's self. This leads us to argue that a truly entrepreneurial theory would be one which seeks to nurture the enterprising capacities of the other.

The concluding chapter of this book asks the question of what remains. We argue that after working through a critique of the entrepreneur, there is still an open question about what exactly is still available. We argue that despite the many queries around the entrepreneur, there is still a promise in this character. We seek to draw out the promise that still remains at the heart of an (albeit radically reconstructed) theory of entrepreneurship. We articulate the outlines of what this might be, and what difference it makes for researchers, policy makers and entrepreneurs. Ultimately, this chapter will gesture towards a more generalised, exciting and responsible theory and practice of entrepreneurship.

2. For a critical theory of entrepreneurship

When the word 'entrepreneur' is used, we often think of the typical 'self-made man' who spotted a gap in the market, started a business, and made it into a large going-concern. Today the word seems to be used in an extremely promiscuous way. It is possible to talk about an employee pursuing a new idea as an 'intrapreneur' (Kanter, 1990). It makes sense to talk about a woman who owns a cow in an Indian village and sells some of the precious milk to her neighbours as a 'micro-entrepreneur' (Westall et al., 2000). A public sector employee who has an eye for gaining funding from the private sector is also an entrepreneur (Osborne and Gaebler, 1992). Those who build new institutions are known as 'institutional entrepreneurs' (Dorado, 2005). An individual who changes the direction of political struggles is called a 'political entrepreneur' (Schneider and Teske, 1992). The ancient activity of charity is now 'social entrepreneurship' (Austin et al., 2006). Professionals such as doctors and nurses have now been recoded as entrepreneurs (Doolin, 2002). This has all led some social critics to argue that we are experiencing a profound and notable generalisation of the category of the entrepreneur, to the point where the figure of the entrepreneur can be used to refer not just to someone undertaking a small business start-up, but to nearly anyone.

In this chapter we ask how we can adequately understand this generalisation of the entrepreneur. We argue that functionalist and interpretive approaches to entrepreneurship are largely inadequate for understanding such a generalisation. This leads us to turn towards more recent critical approaches to entrepreneurship which seek to explore how entrepreneurship creates relations of power and domination.

We will argue that critical approaches to entrepreneurship have yielded some important insights into its generalisation, particularly through the rise of so-called 'cultures of enterprise' (for example du Gay, 1996). However, we note that these studies have not gone far enough. In particular we identify and seek to address a series of vital shortcomings in critical theories of the entrepreneur. By doing this we seek to offer a more comprehensive 'critical theory of entrepreneurship' that will be deployed throughout the book.

FUNCTIONALIST APPROACHES

Until relatively recently, the dominant approach to entrepreneurship was to treat it as an economic function that produced utility. While the term entrepreneur has a long history in economic thought, which will be discussed in more detail in Chapter 4, it is only in the work of Schumpeter (1934) that entrepreneurship becomes an economic factor that produces utility on its own accord. He famously argued that the entrepreneur is the dynamic force in the capitalist economic system which otherwise tends towards stability. The entrepreneur introduces this degree of dynamism by creating new combinations of the factors of production. By doing this, the entrepreneur produces additional value and is rewarded for this added valued by 'entrepreneurial profit'. The unique insight here is that the entrepreneur creates additional utility that does not spring forth from the traditional factors of production – land, labour and capital.

Having identified the economic function of the entrepreneur, a whole field of research has appeared that seeks to explain what mechanisms produce entrepreneurship. Psychologists have sought to locate explanations of entrepreneurship in a set of personality traits such as 'need for achievement' (for example Shaver and Scott, 1991). Sociologists have sought to explore some of the 'structural' factors that might drive or at least facilitate entrepreneurialism (for reviews see Aldrich, 2005; Ruef and Lounsbury, 2007; Swedberg, 2000; Thornton, 1999). Some researchers have identified factors at the firm level, such as a relatively flat organisational structure, policies which allow employees free time to pursue innovative ideas, incentive structures for entrepreneurialism, and firm-wide cultures of innovation. Other factors have been identified at field level such as the stage in a life cycle of a certain industry, the spatial proximity of firms, the density of links between firms, and the existence of field-level institutions. Finally some factors have been identified at policy level including the availability of seed-corn funding, the willingness of financiers or the state to invest in entrepreneurship, and government tax policies (see, for example, Shane, 2003).

These studies have yielded some important results, particularly in relation to the structures that facilitate entrepreneurship. But this search is underpinned by a *functionalist* conception of entrepreneurship. This involves treating entrepreneurship primarily as something that produces economic or social utility. The result is that the focus of such research is the successful entrepreneurial capitalist. This is fatally flawed for a number of reasons. First, as we have noted, many of the actors who are identified today as entrepreneurs are not the owner-manager capitalists that Schumpeter had in mind. Rather they are 'intrapreneurs', 'public sector entrepreneurs', 'institutional entrepreneurs', 'social entrepreneurs' and so on. By holding fast to such a narrow definition of who the entrepreneur might be, we effectively ignore all these other entrepreneurs who are not in business. Second, many entrepreneurs who are in fact 'in business' are often far from successful. As every student of entrepreneurship knows, the huge majority of small businesses fail. Indeed, most entrepreneurs produce the absolute opposite of utility. Entrepreneurs actually systematically destroy utility, as we will show in Chapter 5. To only admit successful entrepreneurs into consideration involves ignoring the silent majority of unsuccessful entrepreneurs. Third, functionalist studies have repeatedly tried and failed to meaningfully identify the variables associated with entrepreneurship as we will discuss in the next chapter. Attempts to identify the personality characteristics and the structural determinates of entrepreneurship have produced inconclusive results (Bygrave, 1989a, 1989b). This has led to a widespread lament that 'the study of entrepreneurship is still in its infancy' (Brazeal and Herbert, 1999: 29). Fourth, functionalist studies have set out to predict situations where entrepreneurship will take off, but they have been largely unsuccessful in this undertaking. This is evident in the fact that entrepreneurship often appears in situations where it 'should not' occur, such as the highly entrepreneurial behaviour in the form of 'blat' trading circles that appeared in the highly 'un-entrepreneurial' context of Soviet Russia (see Eisenstadt and Roninger, 1981; Rehn and Taalas, 2004a, 2004b).

INTERPRETIVE APPROACHES

The failures of functionalist studies of entrepreneurship have led some researchers to give up the search for the causes and effects of entrepreneurship and instead ask how entrepreneurship comes about in a day-to-day fashion (Hjorth and Steyaert, 2004). This has led some researchers to shift from asking how entrepreneurs create utility to how entrepreneurs create meaning and understanding (Gartner, 1990; 1993). At the heart of this process is the dynamic of the 'social construction of entrepreneurship' (Bouchikhi, 1993; Fletcher, 2003; Downing, 2005). Interpretive approaches focus on the everyday activities associated with doing entrepreneurship, how actors interpret, reflect on, and think about these activities, the ways in which they verbalise these thoughts in stories and narratives, and how these stories become fixed into widespread and widely accepted discourses (Hjorth and Steyaert, 2004). This means treating entrepreneurship as 'a conceptual and linguistic resource through which the meanings of organizational creation and emergence are constructed'

(Fletcher, 2003: 128). According to these researchers, the central task of the entrepreneur is not just the creation of utility through developing new combinations of the factors of production. Rather what the entrepreneur creates is new patterns of meaning and interpretation.

In order to understand how meaning is created in the entrepreneurial process, researchers have investigated three dynamics. The first is how entrepreneurs make sense of the social world they find around them. Building on Austrian economics, researchers working in this tradition have argued that the fulcrum of entrepreneurship is 'alertness' to opportunities in the market (for example Kirzner, 1973, 1997). Entrepreneurship involves perceiving opportunities, acting upon them, and organizing to exploit them (Minniti and Bygrave, 1999; Bygrave and Minniti, 2000; Shane and Venkataraman, 2000). Interpretive researchers have demonstrated how a potential entrepreneur's past experiences shape their perceptual schemes, which will condition the kind of opportunities that an entrepreneur will pursue. For instance, the disciplinary background of entrepreneurs conditions the opportunities they perceive in the market and the kind of venture they will eventually create (Shane, 2003). At the very centre of the entrepreneurial process is an actor's ability to perceive or understand the world in an entrepreneurial fashion. The process of entrepreneurship is therefore as much an act of cognitive gymnastics as it is an economic ability.

A second dynamic identified by interpretive studies of entrepreneurship is the way entrepreneurs make creative use of language and perceptual schemas in their day-to-day activities (for example Pitt, 1998; Hjorth and Steyaert, 2004; Johansson, 2004; Rae, 2004; Down, 2006). Researchers working in this tradition have demonstrated how actors use the language of entrepreneurship and opportunity to 'do things' such as convince a bank manager to finance them or build legitimacy with a potential buyer. For instance, Simon Down (2006) argues that a central aspect of the process of entrepreneurship is the creation of narratives. This involves the articulation of story lines, plots and the use of narrative structure. Using these tools, an entrepreneur is able to create relatively stable and coherent patterns of interpretation and meaning.

Third, interpretive approaches allow us to recognise that entrepreneurs do not only create utility, they also create meaning in the course of their personal activities. By placing this at the centre of the study of entrepreneurship, we are able to trace out how entrepreneurs create meaning through the canny perception of opportunities and the wily use of language and narratives to convince potential investors. By focusing on these interpretive processes, we are able to significantly broaden the scope of studies of entrepreneurship. This is because we are able to treat entrepreneurship as a certain way of creating and using meaning which might be mobilised by considering a whole range of actors from business people through to social entrepreneurs.

By only focusing on the interpretive dimension of entrepreneurship, researchers working in this tradition have largely ignored the fact that entrepreneurship significantly involves political and economic questions, in which being 'entrepreneurial' tends to direct one's attention in a certain way, typically towards seeing the world as one gigantic profit opportunity. Indeed entrepreneurship is not just a way of understanding and experiencing the world – it is also a way of acting upon the world, and being with others. This means that the very dominance of the category of the entrepreneur needs to be explained, and the consequences of entrepreneurship on others comprehended. Furthermore, interpretive studies neglect a proper engagement with exactly who gets included and excluded from being identified as an entrepreneur, and the various struggles which occur around these patterns of inclusion and exclusion. We argue throughout this book that in order to understand these struggles, it is not sufficient merely to attend to the interpretive processes at work. Instead, it is vital that we consider the politics and economics of entrepreneurship. By this we mean the ways in which actual entrepreneurs mobilise and work with relations of power and capital. The politics and economics of entrepreneurship also involve the various struggles that occur around the category of the entrepreneur. In order to unmask the politics and economics of entrepreneurship, we would like to offer a critical theory of entrepreneurship.

CRITICAL APPROACHES

In order to think through the politics and economics of entrepreneurship, researchers have begun to investigate the consequences of the category of the entrepreneur. They have done this by asking not just how entrepreneurs use language to do things, but also how the language of entrepreneurship works. In order to do this, researchers working in the critical tradition have argued that entrepreneurship itself must be thought of as a discourse. By this we mean that entrepreneurship is a set of statements mobilised by actors to produce and reproduce political and economic relations. This means that to properly understand entrepreneurship it is not good enough to only consider the processes of utility production or processes of interpretation. It is also vital that we consider entrepreneurship as a way of talking, a language used by people that produces power relations, and that these power relations may involve problems.

During the 1990s a growing group of researchers sought to examine entrepreneurship as discourse (Hjorth and Steyaert, 2004). They did this first of all in response to what they perceived to be the increasing prevalence of a 'culture of enterprise', which exhorted everyone from small business owners to public servants to act more entrepreneurially (see for example Keat and Abercrombie, 1991). The core characteristics of 'being entrepreneurial' involved being calculating, taking risks, approaching oneself as a business, and seeking out opportunities to make oneself more marketable (Heelas and Morris, 1992). Perhaps the most notable change brought about by the introduction of enterprise culture was a widespread shift in the language used in a whole range of sectors. Socio-linguists such as Norman Fairclough (1995) noted that during the 1980s and 1990s, there was a rapid spread and generalisation of talk about people being entrepreneurial and enterprising. Institutions from schools to hospitals, factories to retail outlets, the development sector and those with environmental concerns came to be infused with the language of enterprise. What is vital here is that these discourses of enterprise represented the entrepreneur as unfailingly positive and were systematically applied as the catch-all solution to almost any aspect of social life.

The rise of enterprise culture did not only involve an innocent change in how we talk about the social world. It also involved more deep-seated political and economic relations. Some researchers argued that perhaps the most important expression of these changing relations were shifts in the way actors understood their very sense of self. Those studying 'governmentality' argued that the rise of entrepreneurship discourse led to actors being positioned as rational self-calculating subjects who weigh up costs and benefits as well as pursuing entrepreneurial opportunities (Rose, 1996; Burchell, 1993; du Gay and Salaman, 1992; Hjorth, 2003). This process of the internalisation of enterprise discourse was examined in a range of studies that demonstrate how workers come to think of themselves as 'enterprising subjects'. For instance, researchers charted the rise of entrepreneurial identities in large corporations (Fournier, 1998), middle management (du Gay et al., 1996; Badham et al., 2003), the professions (Doolin, 2002), the public sector (du Gay, 2003), government policy making (Perren and Jennings, 2005), and society more generally (Ogbor, 2000; Nicholson and Anderson, 2005). Throughout each of these studies, the major point was that the rise of enterprise discourse has led to changes in how employees think about their work and themselves.

This research on enterprise culture has come to some remarkably consistent conclusions. First, it has shown that enterprise is a relatively coherent discourse which emphasises risk taking, calculation and economising, and represents these points in unfailingly positive ways. Second, it has sought to repeatedly argue that enterprise culture has effects that are not just caused by structural changes in multinational capitalism. Rather, it also involves a significant change in the symbolism, understandings, and perceptions of people in an economy. In short, the rise of enterprise culture has a vital and irreducibly cultural dimension. Third, the effects of enterprise culture are largely 'ideational' in nature insofar as they change how people talk and think about themselves and the social world. Finally, the rise of enterprise culture produces important changes in how people understand themselves and what they are able and not able to do. This occurs through the construction of subject positions which carefully delimit the scope of possible action that people can and cannot carry out.

These critical approaches to entrepreneurship certainly make some important additions to existing interpretive work on the topic. This body of work demonstrates that entrepreneurship is more than just a process of making meaning – it is also a process of producing and reproducing relations of domination. Indeed the literature on enterprise culture has convincingly argued that the language of enterprise has spread throughout various sectors of the economy and in some cases transformed how we can operate and speak. However, some queries can be raised about significant shortcomings in the critical literature on enterprise culture.

The first question is about exactly how 'coherent' the discourse of enterprise is. As we will argue in the next chapter, the discourse of entrepreneurship contains an essential and inescapable ambiguity. That is, the language of enterprise is not a complete and coherent package but is punctuated by holes, ambiguities, and gaps. Indeed, the essentially ambiguous nature of entrepreneurship makes the entrepreneur a mythical and unworldly character.

The second question is how 'ideational' the changes associated with enterprise culture actually are. A number of researchers have argued that the appearance of discourses of enterprise often has important dimensions that are not totally reducible to discourse (see for example Armstrong, 2001; see also Reed, 2000). These include changes in the way rules are structured as well as the distribution of resources. By ignoring this important 'extra-discursive' dimension, researchers have been unable to document how changes in discourse might also be connected or indeed embodied within shifts in the distribution of more material configurations.

The third major question is whether there are any structural factors that determine who can use enterprise discourse and who cannot. That is, if we took this research at its word, would this mean that a simple change in the language would be enough to make someone into an entrepreneur? This effectively writes out of the account various structural factors such as state policy, the dynamics of capital and the nature of kinship relations in a society that might make entrepreneurship discourse more desirable in some cases and less in others. It also leads us to ignore how an individual's structural position may make them more or less likely to be able to don the mantle of being an entrepreneur.

The final question is exactly how constrained actors who are 'made up' or produced by discourses of enterprise are (Fournier and Grey, 1999). Many studies of enterprise culture assume a relatively 'strong' account of discourse that focuses on how enterprise limits the way in which people can talk and understand themselves. By focusing too much on moments of closure and limitation, critics of enterprise culture blind themselves to the way that the language of enterprise may be used creatively, tactically and ingeniously (see for example Hjorth, 2005).

REWORKING A CRITICAL THEORY OF THE ENTREPRENEUR

In order to address these four questions put to critical approaches to entrepreneurship, we will turn to some of the tenets underlying the emerging general tendency of critical management studies. Critical management studies is a growing tradition that has called into question the objectivity and politically neutral assumptions that underscore the bulk of work on questions related to management (for surveys see Alvesson et al., 2009; Grey and Willmott, 2005). Critical management studies has broadly sought to highlight the processes of domination central to organisational life. Early attempts to sketch out a critical study of management and organisation were tempered by the environmentalist and humanist reactions to technocracy during the 1960s (for example Marcuse, 1964; Scott, 1974). This stream of thought emphasised processes of organisational decay, scarcity and dissent in place of the dominant fascination with organisational growth, abundance and consensus. Central to this was a call for management researchers to abandon dominant approaches associated with functionalism and become more attuned to the 'darker side' of organisations, in particular issues of domination. Later work developed this account of domination in organisations by drawing on a lineage of Marxist thought to chart processes that render 'social arrangements which seem fixed and permanent (as) temporary, arbitrary patterns and any observed social patterns are regarded as one among many possibilities' (Benson, 1977: 3). This also involved a commitment to the practice of 'free and creative reconstruction of social arrangements on the basis of a reasoned analysis of both the limits and potentials of present social forms' (p. 5). Instead of labouring under technical interests and aiming to control nature and people, or working with practical interests that aimed to develop hermeneutic and historical understandings of a specific situation, a critical study of organisation would attempt to develop emancipatory knowledge (Habermas, 1972; Stablein and Nord, 1985). This knowledge would be emancipatory insofar as it aims to develop freedom and responsibility by challenging regimes of domination.

A critical theory of the entrepreneur therefore seeks to call into question the regimes of domination that are constructed and perpetuated under the name of the entrepreneur. The aim of this questioning would be to unsettle these forms of domination in order to create space for configuring more free and reasoned social relationships. In what follows we argue that this project of critique would have four strands that together contribute to this objective. These are: (1) the critique of representation, (2) the critique of affects, (3) the critique of structural limitations and (4) the critique of agency. The remainder of this chapter stretches the broad outlines of the critical theory of entrepreneurship that we deploy in this book, and in the remaining chapters we will set these critiques to work.

CRITIQUE OF REPRESENTATION

The first problem we need to point to is a tendency to see enterprise discourse as a whole, a unity that is more or less enclosed, stable and comprehensible. This is a basic idea that we find across a range of competing 'definitions' of discourse (see, for example, Phillips et al., 2004), in which discourses are, for example, 'structured collections of meaningful texts' or 'systems of statements which construct an object' (Parker, 1992: 5). The persistence of the idea of discursive unity, even in those claiming to draw on the work of Foucault is rather odd. In many discourse analyses, we find the recurrence of phrases from Foucault such as 'set of statements' or 'discursive regularities', but these phrases are dragged out of the context in which Foucault proposed them and are used to consolidate the idea that discourse is a constituted unity which then acts in certain ways – to exercise power, to create subjects, and so on. If we look at a book like the *Archaeology of Knowledge*, the work in which Foucault made his most sustained effort to engage with methodological questions regarding the analyses of discourse, we find much that rubs against the idea that discourse is a unified set of statements. Rather, presupposed unities must be called into question:

These pre-existing forms of continuity, all these syntheses that are accepted without question, must remain in suspense. They must not be rejected definitively of course, but the tranquillity with which they are accepted must be disturbed; we must show that they do not come about by themselves, but are always the result of a construction the rules of which must be known. (Foucault, 1972: 25)

The point here is that the assumption of unity, either at the level of discourse or rules of discursive formation, creates a number of problems, some of which we will further exemplify in the following chapters. But to put it in simple terms, assuming the unity of a discourse (1) presses definition onto statements in such a way that it misses too much of the heterogeneity of a discourse like entrepreneurship; (2) gives too much credit to the unity of what is said and what it means; and (3) leads to certain ways of thinking of resistance, in which resistance is treated as external to this constituted unity, rather than immanent to it.

For these reasons, we need to think about discourse in slightly more complex ways. This involves Foucault's important cautions about the unity of discourse, and also involves, particularly in the next chapter, some ideas from Jacques Lacan's conception of language. What is important for our immediate purpose is how Lacan offers a way of thinking about the stability and coherence of discourse. In this we face the question of linguistic structures, or what Lacan calls 'the Symbolic' in relation to that which is inexpressible in language, or what Lacan calls 'the Real'.

Most important for our purposes is Lacan's insistence that attempts at symbolisation are always under threat, and in this sense the Real is that which interrupts the Symbolic. This is a notion which is both prosaic and profound. In a simple sense, it is to say that we can't say everything, that there are some things we have trouble saying. More radically, the discovery of the Real means that all claims about the coherence of language are threatened by the failure of language. It is this radical consequence that is, for Slavoj Žižek, the important result of the Lacanian category of the Real. As he puts it:

Today, it is a commonplace that the Lacanian subject is divided, crossed-out, identical to a lack in the signifying chain. However, the most radical dimension of Lacanian theory lies not in recognizing this fact but in realizing that the big Other, the symbolic order itself, is also *barré*, crossed-out, by a fundamental impossibility, structured around an impossible/traumatic kernel, around a central lack. (Žižek, 1989: 122)

The consequences of a Lacanian conception of language are many. First, as we argue in the next chapter, a Lacanian understanding results in a suspicion of the force of language, and in particular of the idea that subjects can be thoroughly constituted in language. To put this in Lacanian jargon, the Real presents a traumatic kernel which resists an enclosed or final capture by the Symbolic. But further to this, and more important for our argument here, Lacan reminds us that language does not always gain its efficacy from its completeness or coherence. Lacan can powerfully draw attention to the operation of language not as a force that is effective because of its stability, but on the contrary can be effective exactly when it is unstable, diffuse and decentred. This is not to argue that coherent and well-formed discourses cannot be ideologically effective. They can. But it is to remind us that language does not always work in the same way. It can work due to its consistency, but it can also operate due to its inconsistency (Eagleton, 1991). Lacan is not suggesting that language is always inconsistent, but he has some useful ways of understanding discourse which break with the assumptions of logical form that we find behind the assumption that entrepreneurship discourse is effective because it is a well-coordinated set of statements.

The operation of discourse in this way can be seen in Lacan's notions of the empty signifier which rests at the 'absent centre' of a symbolic system (see Laclau, 1996; Žižek, 1999). When a language is organised around an unstable or mobile centre, this discourse offers itself to being assembled in a variety of different ways. If a variety of discursive elements can be quilted together by a central nodal point and that nodal point is itself subject to semiotic slippage, then what appears to be the 'same' discourse can be articulated in a number of different ways by different participants, all of whom may be using the 'same' language, but with different meanings and different consequences.

CRITIQUE OF AFFECTS

This leads us to the second strand of our outline of a critical theory of entrepreneurship, which is the question of consciousness. Work examining enterprise discourse often assumes that subjects are constructed in relation to language. When these identities are formed, or these subjects are constructed, action takes place on the basis of discourse. So discourse initiates action, and it does this by passing through the consciousness of subjects. This is a recurrent problem in social theory, and a problem in the analysis of entrepreneurship discourse. In this regard we might recall the important critique of the 'dominant ideology thesis' outlined by Nicholas Abercrombie, Stephen Hill and Bryan Turner (1980). They were faced by an overpowering emphasis on ideology and, in particular, on the notion of a 'dominant ideology' which was being used to explain political power and the persistence of capitalism. Abercrombie et al. made an effective intervention in this debate by recalling Marx's conclusion that the 'dull compulsion of economic relations completes the subjugation of the labourer to the capitalist' (Marx, 1954: 689).

This is to say, many people are not the victims of subjugation by discourse or by having the wrong consciousness. Many people in organisation understand exactly that they are victims of domination, and often can express this very clearly and eloquently, the thing being that they are faced by an economic power against which it is very hard to effect resistance, and against which much presses in the direction of capitulation. Their thoughts and discourse may be at odds with their action, but this is not a deficit on the side of their consciousness, it is a practical obstacle, one that we also call power.

So by learning the importance of language from interpretive approaches we can also put language in its place in relation to political and economic forces. We can then 'think' language again, but in its materiality and its material imbrications with life. We find a powerful elaboration of such ideas in Deleuze and Guattari's 'postulates of linguistics'. Deleuze and Guattari are forceful in their attempt to think language while seeking to avoid the problems of consciousness. Indeed, they argue that language is not, first and foremost, a matter of communication. We find this in volume one of *Capitalism and Schizophrenia* when they dismantle the notion of the signifier and signification, arguing that the question is not 'what does it mean?' but 'how does it work?'. Thus, they propose to think language, desire and capital in terms of machinic connections (1983: 109). In their book on Kafka they also stress their objection to models of meaning, claiming that they 'believe only in a Kafka *politics* that is neither imaginary nor symbolic. We believe only in one or more Kafka *machines*' (1986: 7). And in volume two of *Capitalism and Schizophrenia* they begin their discussion of the postulates by destroying the claim that 'language is informational and communicational', using the example of education:

> When the schoolmistress instructs her students on a rule of grammar or arithmetic, she is not informing them, any more than she is informing herself when she questions a student. She does not so much instruct as 'insign', give orders or commands. A teacher's commands are not external or additional to what he or she teaches us. They do not flow from primary significations or result from information: an order always and already concerns prior orders, which is why ordering is redundancy. The compulsory education machine does not communicate information; it imposes upon the child semiotic coordinates possessing all of the dual foundations of grammar (masculine-feminine, singular-plural,

noun-verb, subject of the statement-subject of the enunciation, etc.). The elementary unit of language – the statement – is the order-word (Deleuze and Guattari, 1988: 75–76).

In Deleuze and Guattari we find a radical emphasis on the attempt, on the part of language, to do something quite different from communication or meaning. They offer this in a radically compressed form in their aphorism: 'Language is not made to be believed but to be obeyed, and to compel obedience' (1988: 76). The consequences of such a reframing of language are, no doubt, profound, as they put into question all of the notions which we find so easy about meaning and sense. One can only imagine how radically this disrupts the notions which are unchallenged – nay, unconsidered – in Karl Weick's otherwise important analyses of sensemaking in organizations (Weick, 1995, 2001). While we have no hopes at all that Deleuze and Guattari could be easily assimilated into the analysis of entrepreneurship discourse (for an explanation of why Deleuze and Guattari are by definition inassimilable see Sørensen, 2005), in our work we find possibilities for a thinking of language as mobilisation and connection/disconnection, without an arbitrary privilege of either consciousness or language.

CRITIQUE OF STRUCTURAL LIMITATIONS

The third strand in our proposed critical theory of entrepreneurship involves questions of the 'extra-discursive' factors that structure the context in which these discourses appear. The result of privileging language often results in losing sight of political and economic relations, and for this reason, a turn to language and a concomitant disavowal of things extra-discursive have been roundly criticised (Ackroyd and Fleetwood, 2000; Armstrong, 2001; Reed, 1998, 2000, 2009). An analysis of discourse cannot alone account for the enduring social structures such as the state or capitalism. Mike Reed has argued that a discursive approach to power relations effectively blinds critical theorists to issues of social structures:

> Foucauldian discourse analysis is largely restricted to a tactical and localised view of power, as constituted and expressed through situational-specific 'negotiated orders', which seriously underestimates the structural reality of more permanent and hierarchal power relations. It finds it difficult, if not impossible, to deal with institutionalised stabilities and continuities in power relations because it cannot get at the higher levels of social organisation in which micro-level processes and practices are embedded. (Reed, 2000: 526–7)

These institutional stabilities may include market relations, the power of the state, relations like colonialism, kinship and patriarchy. These are the 'generative properties' that Reed (1998: 210) understands as 'mak(ing) social practices and forms – such as discursive formations – what they are and equip(ing) them with what they do'. Equally Thompson and Ackroyd also argue that in discourse analysis 'workers are not disciplined by the market, or sanctions actually or potentially invoked by capital, but their own subjectivities' (1995: 627). The inability to examine structures such as capitalism means that some basic forms of power are thus uninvestigated. Focusing solely on entrepreneurship discourse within organisations and the workplace would lead to a situation where pertinent relations that do not enter into discourse are taken to not exist. Such oversights in discursive analyses are that often structural relations such as class and the state have become so reified in social and mental worlds that they disappear. An ironic outcome indeed. Even when this structural context is considered, it is often examined in broad, oversimplified, and underspecified manners. This attention to social structure can be an important part of developing a critical theory of entrepreneurship, as we remember that the existing structural arrangements at any point are not inevitable, but can be subjected to criticism and change.

In order to deal with these problems, we need to revive the concept of social structure. Thus we are arguing that 'there exist in the social world itself and not only within symbolic systems (language, myths, etc.) objective structures independent of the consciousness and will of agents, which are capable of guiding and constraining their practices or their representations' (Bourdieu, 1990: 122). Objective still means socially constructed, but social constructions that have become solidified as structures external to individual subjects. Examples of these structures may include basic 'organising principals' which are relatively stable and spatially and historically situated such as capitalism, kinship, patriarchy and the state. Some entrepreneurship researchers, particularly those drawing on sociology and political science, have shown the importance of social structure for understanding entrepreneurship (see for example Swedberg, 2000).

CRITIQUE OF AGENCY

The question of agency is in many ways the flipside of structure. As we have noted above, many of the criticisms of studies of enterprise culture have focused on the lacking account of agency. These critics have argued that actors who are faced with efforts to promulgate enterprise discourse in their workplaces do not automatically adopt these discourses (Armstrong,

2005). These discourses do not simply construct a subject position which actors automatically and wilfully take up. Rather, in reality entrepreneurship is often treated with a significant degree of circumspection if not outright cynicism by the intended targets.

One way that critical researchers have sought to build an account of agency back into studies of enterprise culture has been to look at use of language. To do so involves rejecting the assumption that subjects are completely positioned by the political and economic relations they find themselves in. Instead, it seeks to show how enterprise culture is practically achieved through day-to-day interaction (see Cohen and Musson, 2002). According to this approach, it is only in and through the practical exercises of using discourse that enterprise discourse takes on any social reality. Researchers have used this strategy to show how actors may use entrepreneurship discourse to achieve a whole range of practical goals from supporting relatively unrelated arguments through to simply silencing an opponent in conversation. The central point here is that entrepreneurship discourse can, and indeed consistently is pressed into the service of many different actors to achieve their own relatively mundane projects.

Another variant of this approach is employed by those who seek to locate agency in the tactical appropriation and consumption of discourse. Drawing on de Certeau's notion of tactics, Hjorth (2005) has argued that enterprise discourse is actively and knowingly 'consumed' by its intended recipients (see also Fournier and Grey, 1999). Through this process of consumption, recipients are able to attribute meanings to discourses which are not intended by the original issuer. For instance, discourses of entrepreneurship have been pressed into service by North American rap artists to shift their image from being potential welfare cases to being esteemed and valued members of society (Sköld and Rehn, 2007). By using discourses of entrepreneurship in such an unlikely way these same rap artists have been able to twist and reconfigure just what might be meant by the figure of the entrepreneur. The central point here is that through active and tactical use of the discourse of enterprise this discourse can be reconfigured and reformulated.

Other researchers have sought inspiration from the growing body of research on workplace resistance (see Fleming and Spicer, 2007). They sought to trace the rejection of entrepreneurship discourses both in the workplace and at large. They have found that this rejection might take a number of forms. In some cases, the introduction of an entrepreneurship discourse might give rise to a gentle and somewhat playful ironic humour (Badham et al., 2003). These humorous engagements do not seek however to actively and directly challenge enterprise culture. Some researchers have reported a militant rejection of enterprise culture on the part of some workers in favour of more technocratic identities (Fournier, 1998). In each of these studies, we find repeated again and again that the introduction of an enterprise culture programme does not necessarily equate with immediate employee take-up. In fact, it appears that ritualised humour and cynicism seems to be an integral aspect of enterprise culture. We might even go so far as to suggest that it is precisely this cynical distance towards enterprise culture that makes it work (Fleming and Spicer, 2003).

Perhaps the most recent strand of literature on this topic shows that there are a number of attempts to articulate discourses in relation to entrepreneurship. For instance, Paul du Gay's (2000b, 2004) work has sought to put forward an argument for the ethos of bureaucracy in place of the ethos of enterprise in the public sector. Others have found social movements contesting the rise of entrepreneurialism in a public broadcaster that actively articulated alternative discourses such as 'national culture' and 'government accountability' in the face of the rising influence of entrepreneurship (Spicer and Fleming, 2007). The central point here is that enterprise discourse may not just be challenged through tactical engagement or rejection – it can, and indeed is challenged through full frontal attack.

Ultimately, the question of agency has led us to ask critically whether employees are subjected to enterprise discourse. We have seen that at the very least actors participate in the active construction of their subjectivities. In fact, in many cases talk of entrepreneurship may simply be a sideshow to more important and immediate practical struggles around who gets to talk or who gets a planning permit. In some cases, it may be vital to trace out how entrepreneurship discourse is actively challenged, resisted and in some cases destroyed. By paying attention to the active contests around enterprise discourse we begin to become aware that the entrepreneurial subject is not simply given – rather it is a terrain of struggle, resistance and power.

THE TASK AHEAD

What then would a critical theory of entrepreneurship look like? Such a theory would be primarily driven by an emancipatory intent. Critical studies of entrepreneurship seek to free us from ill-considered ideas and politico-economic regimes of domination. This stands in marked contrast to functionalist approaches, which seek to achieve efficiency and effectiveness, and also to interpretive approaches, which seek merely to understand entrepreneurship. A critical theory of entrepreneurship involves the effort to question the assumed stability of the category of the entrepreneur. This involves showing how the entrepreneur is not a necessary or universal character, but a historically and spatially specific figure who is implicated in relations of domination. In order to do so, a critical theory of the entrepreneur investigates the role of political struggles in the process of entrepreneurship and the place of entrepreneurship in broader social and political struggles. A critical theory of entrepreneurship also acknowledges the way that forms of academic knowledge and understanding are bound up with the relations of domination associated with the entrepreneur. Failure to critically reflect on relations of domination implicated with entrepreneurship is in this way a failure of any academic inquiry into entrepreneurship.

We are therefore proposing a fundamental change in the study of entrepreneurship, instead of just seeking to understand how actors make sense of particular situations by using notions of entrepreneurship, and by focusing on the politics of enterprise. By this we mean that a critical theory of entrepreneurship investigates the political and economic consequences of entrepreneurship. This involves examination of why some may get referred to as entrepreneurs and why others may not, what kind of power relations this creates, and how this power works.

In developing this critique of entrepreneurship, we are not simply proposing the negative goal of criticising and ultimately eliminating the category of entrepreneurship from language. That is, we are not just seeking to point out how the character of the entrepreneur is 'bad'. Rather what we are suggesting is an affirmative critique which involves the active reuse and reanimation of the term. This involves the affirmative task of how we can radically extend the concept of entrepreneurship. Through this act of radical extension we might change what is meant by entrepreneurship, hence extending the project of 'rewriting entrepreneurship' (Hjorth, 2003). This would involve the task of taking hold of the significant creative potential that rests within people who are not recognised as being entrepreneurial. To recognise this creativity involves radically changing what we mean by the entrepreneur and who it is that gets to be one – this would involve the kind of radical extension of the idea of enterprising which Daniel Hjorth and others are already pursuing (for example, Hjorth, 2003; Hjorth and Steyaert, 2009a; Hjorth et al., 2008, Bill, 2006). From where we stand, such a radical extension would recognise that the task ahead of us is no longer to interpret entrepreneurship, but rather to change it.

3. The sublime object of entrepreneurship

One of the major questions in this book is: when we use the word entrepreneur, what on earth do we mean? This question is typically sidestepped or treated as a technical matter by functionalist approaches. Building on the interpretive tradition, we need to understand what 'entrepreneurship' means. But we need to move beyond merely interpreting the entrepreneur, and pose this question in a more critical way. When we do this, we will find that entrepreneurship discourse has been constantly unable to assign a positive identity to the character of the entrepreneur. Shifting away from stable categories, we propose in this chapter a preliminary unmasking, in which the entrepreneur is no longer a stable thing, but a phantasmatic category, a sublime object.

In doing so we draw on the work of Jacques Lacan, which we briefly introduced in the previous chapter. We suggest that a broadly Lacanian conception of the relation between the subject and language might offer a way out of some of the impasses which currently puzzle those concerned with understanding the enterprising subject. We work through these general claims by focusing on the specific case of the operation of discourses of enterprise, their effects in the constitution of enterprising subjects, and problems around the category of 'the entrepreneur'. We begin with a discussion of one exemplary critical study of enterprise – Paul du Gay's examination of enterprise culture. Du Gay's work and subsequent responses to it can be read as a significant moment in debates around how enterprise discourse hails subjects, who then further the cause of post-industrial capital through their own volition.

THE LIMITS OF ENTERPRISE CULTURE

Du Gay is one of the most important critics of the concept of enterprise culture. In his analysis, he has provided an account of the consequences for 'the construction of new work identities and the production of different work-based subjects' (1996: 3; see also du Gay and Salaman, 1992; du Gay, 1991; 1994; 1996; 2000b; 2004). At first glance the theoretical frame is broadly Foucauldian: enterprise appears in the form of a discourse which enacts relations of power through the construction of subject positions, in a process which involves 'making up' enterprising subjects.

In responding to du Gay's work, Fournier and Grey (1999) raise a number of criticisms (see also Fournier, 1998; Armstrong, 2001). While their criticisms are wide-ranging, of interest here are their comments about subjectivity and their charge that du Gay offers 'too little' of an account of resistance and of alternative discourses to enterprise. They assert, in short, that in du Gay's work 'enterprise is treated deterministically' (Fournier and Grey, 1999: 117). In doing so Fournier and Grey evoke the now wide-spread criticism of Foucauldian studies discussed in the previous chapter, on the basis that it denies, or at least displays a tendency to neglect, the possibility of agency and resistance (see, for example, Gabriel, 1999; Newton, 1998; Reed, 1998, 2000; Thompson and Ackroyd, 1995).

Fournier and Grey's case is more sophisticated, and indeed more para-doxical, than a simple dismissal of du Gay's analysis of enterprise on the grounds that his Foucauldianism leads him to ignore resistance. They insist that a Foucauldian approach is not necessarily inimical to accounts of resistance, and hence try to avoid the simplifying and ultimately disap-pointing rejection of Foucault that we find in critics such as Thompson and Ackroyd, who suggest that 'neglect of resistance . . . reflects the limi-tation of Foucault's analysis where, in the desire to avoid explanations at the level of the subject, human agency gets lost in the constitution of the subject solely through discourse' (1995: 625). Indeed, what we find inter-esting in Fournier and Grey's criticism is the paradoxical and equivocal nature of their charges against du Gay, which offer themselves for closer scrutiny.

While Fournier and Grey argue that du Gay fails to account for resist-ance, they are faced with the problem, which they admit, that du Gay *does* in fact attempt to offer an account of resistance to enterprise discourse. In his response to Fournier and Grey, du Gay insists: 'I have gone out of my way to indicate on a number of occasions, both theoretically and empiri-cally, the impossibility of eradicating difference, diversity and antagonism from organizational relations' (du Gay, 2000a: 178). Fournier and Grey concede that du Gay does 'attempt' to account for resistance, citing him when he writes that:

> While the official discourse of enterprise tries to produce particular meanings for and forms of conduct among employees that will in turn produce quality service for customers and a sale for the company, it cannot completely close off the processes of the production of meaning nor totally determine how par-ticular norms will be enacted. (du Gay, 1996: 160, cited by Fournier and Grey, 1999: 199)

Fournier and Grey suggest that du Gay 'escapes complete determinism and makes space for resistance' (1999: 120) by turning to the sphere of consumption, but conclude that du Gay's analysis of consumption ultimately fails to reintroduce resistance. The problem with such an argument is that it fails to recognise that it is not through a turn to relations of consumption that du Gay seeks to 'escape determinism' but that du Gay introduces motifs of resistance by turning, at crucial points, to a quite different theoretical source. To put it bluntly, Fournier and Grey too easily assume that du Gay simply adopts a Foucauldian view of the subject, and in doing so they fail to notice when du Gay draws on quite different sources. Compared to his earlier articles, Fournier and Grey argue:

> In *Consumption and Identity at Work*, du Gay presents a less deterministic view of enterprise; he draws on Foucault to suggest that no discourse or mode of rationality is complete or has complete power over its subjects. He admits the impossibility of one form of government to capture the real, so that 'government is a congenitally failing operation'. (Fournier and Grey, 1999: 119)

Let us follow the twists and turns of du Gay's text more closely. Directly following the comment 'government is a congenitally failing operation' in *Consumption and Identity at Work*, du Gay explains, writing: 'The "Real" always escapes attempts to govern it because there is always a "surplus" separating the "Real" from its symbolization' (du Gay, 1996: 73). Now, the problem is that this is not Foucauldian language. Indeed, du Gay's capitalisation and insertion in quotation marks of 'the Real' (which strangely disappears when Fournier and Grey mention it) is far from accidental but makes explicit reference to Lacan's quite specific conception of 'the Real'. Indeed, the Real is a central concept for Lacan – we might even say that it is *the* Lacanian concept *par excellence*. As his son-in-law Jacques-Alain Miller explains:

> The term 'real', which was at first of only minor importance, acting as a kind of safety rail, has gradually been developed, and its signification has been considerably altered. It began, naturally enough, by presenting, in relation to the symbolic substitutions and imaginary variations, a function of constancy: 'the real is that which always returns to the same place'. It then became that before which the imaginary faltered, that over which the symbolic stumbles, that which is refractory, resistant. Hence the formula: 'the real is the impossible'. It is in this sense that the term begins to appear regularly, as an adjective, to describe that which is lacking in the symbolic order, the ineliminable residue of all articulation, the foreclosed element, which may be approached, but never grasped: the umbilical cord of the symbolic. (Miller, 1977: x)

This reference to Lacan is quite explicit in du Gay, and we find an outline of a range of Lacanian concepts in the pages which run up to the section cited by Fournier and Grey (du Gay, 1996: 70–73). In these pages du Gay outlines some of the basic formulae of a Lacanian conception of the social, and hence argues that 'all attempts to capture the "Real" symbolically ultimately fail. There is always a "left-over", a "surplus" separating the "Real" from its symbolization' (du Gay, 1996: 70). Let us be clear – the source of this jargon comes via Lacan, not Foucault. Here du Gay draws on Žižek as well as Laclau and Mouffe, writers who are all significantly influenced by Lacan. This 'ineradicable surplus' is described by du Gay, following Žižek (1989) as a 'traumatic real kernel', and following Laclau and Mouffe (1985) as an ineradicable 'antagonism' (du Gay, 1996: 71). Paraphrasing Laclau and Mouffe, du Gay finds that contradiction and resistance are inherent in any social system because '"the social" is "always an inconsistent field structured around a constitutive impossibility" a fundamental antagonism' (du Gay, 1996: 71, cf. Laclau and Mouffe, 1985: 125–127).

Even with these brief indications from the text, it should be clear that du Gay has a 'theoretical safeguard' from determinism, which appears not in a turn to consumption but in the category of the Real which he borrows from Lacan. His references in these crucial sections are not to Foucault (as is suggested by Fournier and Grey) but to Lacan, and to 'Lacanians', specifically Žižek and Laclau and Mouffe. When Fournier and Grey argue that du Gay 'draws on *Foucault* to suggest that no discourse or mode of rationality is complete or has complete power over its subjects' (Fournier and Grey, 1999: 119, emphasis added) they fail to acknowledge the preceding section of du Gay's work and in doing so fail to be clear about the moments in which du Gay turns, not to Foucault, but to Lacan and the Lacanian tradition. It is this latter tradition which we propose is vital for understanding organisational life and entrepreneurship in particular (see also Cederström and Hoedemaekers, forthcoming; *Organization*, forthcoming).

OUTING LACAN

When we say that in du Gay there is a tension between a Foucauldian and a Lacanian conception of the subject, this is not to say that du Gay is a 'closet Lacanian', which might imply that there is a genuine Lacanianism which could be found behind his Foucauldian veneer. Rather, it is to say that his text is drawn in two directions, caught between two determinations and unable to decide conclusively in one direction or the other. Further, taking into account the marginal position of Lacanian analyses of economic questions it is not totally surprising that the Lacanian influence went unremarked by Fournier and Grey. While Lacan has had a significant impact on cultural and social theory, his work has until recently largely been unexplored in studies of entrepreneurship and organisations (cf. Arnaud, 2002; Contu, 2008; Driver, 2008; Jones, 2007; Roberts, 2005; Stavrakakis, 2008; Vanheule et al., 2003). Even when addressing issues which are of central concern to Lacan such as the subject and language, there has been a tendency to privilege Foucauldian frames of reference. We can see this here in an extreme form, when the Lacanian influence on du Gay's work passes without comment under the critical gaze of Fournier and Grey.

Here we join with others who have found it productive to draw on Lacan in order to address questions of political and economic analysis. As Lacanian analysis of entrepreneurship is rare, to say the least, it is perhaps a good idea to clarify what we hope to take from Lacan. Importantly, while Arnaud (2002), Vanheule et al. (2003) and Roberts (2005) elect to conduct organisational analyses using the concepts of the Imaginary and the Symbolic, we will here emphasise the Real, which is the third and possibly most disruptive element of Lacan's theoretical triangle. The Real is also the element to which du Gay explicitly refers, and which we will use in the course of this chapter in our attempt to unmask the phantasmic character of the entrepreneur.

We are more than aware of certain limitations in Lacan's work, most obvious of which is his sometimes excessive writing style, something about which we should be alert, even if we do not feel inclined to disparage this as an 'art of evasion' (Derrida, 1981: 110). More problematic perhaps is his troubled relationship with feminism, which results in part from Lacan's often over-enthusiastic identification with Freud and the patriarchal stain that this leaves across Lacan's work. Anyone hoping to engage with Lacan must face up to this stain, although we do not think that a stained carpet is necessarily a useless one (see also Grosz, 1990). In the light of such problems, and drawing critically on the work of Lacanian critics such as Brennan (1993), Copjec (1994), Salecl (1998) and in particular Žižek (1989, 1997, 1999), we propose to engage with Lacan in order to address specific questions of subjectivity and enterprise, while remaining cautious of this endeavour, and of previous discussions of Lacan. This is not a marketing exercise on Lacan's behalf. But first, because Lacanian jargon is not generally taken as legal tender in studies of entrepreneurship, perhaps we should move to explain some basic principles, and clarify some basic misunderstandings.

BEYOND THE MIRROR STAGE . . . AND BACK

When Lacan has been taken up in management and organisation studies, it has often been through discussion of the concept of 'the mirror stage', which appears in his early paper 'The Mirror Stage as Formative of the *I*

Function as Revealed in Psychoanalytic Experience' (in Lacan, 2006a, first published 1937). In this paper Lacan tells the parable of the act of a young child who, from about the age of six months, becomes able to recognise its own image reflected back to it. The child 'who has not yet mastered walking, or even standing [and] still trapped in his motor impotence and nursling dependence' is able to fixate on its image, in an act of what we know as *identification* (Lacan, 2006a: 75–76). This early experience is, for Lacan, central to the formation of self, and is a central metaphor in his early work, which focuses on what he calls 'Imaginary' relations, the relations of identification of a subject with an image.

If we were to go no further we would find here the Hegelian motif of the development of self-consciousness, the story of the subject coming to know itself by being recognised in the eyes of others, which is one of the guiding strands of the *Phenomenology of Spirit* (Hegel, 1977; see also Carr and Zanetti, 1999, Hancock and Tyler, 2001). The mirror stage, in this reduced form, is often taken to be Lacan's contribution, offering a conception of the subject who finds itself mirrored in its relations to others.

It is important that we remember that Lacan offers far more than a model in which the subject recognises itself in the mirror of the social. Indeed, such a model could be easily found in Hegel, in Mead, or in a variety of social psychologies in which the self is socially constructed in its daily interactions with others. Such ideas about self-identification are now common in studies of entrepreneurship (see for example Foss, 2004). Such a model of the subject is a beginning, but it might too easily reduce Lacan to some form of 'social constructivist' in which the relation between the subject and the other is easy and satisfying, and in which the subject 'takes up' a whole and coherent 'identity' in relation to the other.

The mirror stage, for Lacan, is not a comforting discovery. If we go back to the opening of this, his 'first' work, we find Lacan insist that the conception of the mirror stage 'sets us at odds with any philosophy directly stemming from the *cogito*' (2006a: 75). The challenge of the mirror stage is not in seeing the subject as being constructed in relation to the other, a notion which is anyway almost a commonplace today. The challenge is that the act of recognition simultaneously involves a dynamic of misrecognition (see also Althusser, 1971; Pêcheux, 1994). The subject perceives itself as whole, as a bounded and effectively 'good' entity surrounded by the evils of the world. This is the self-satisfying image of a coherent subject in which, as Lacan puts it 'the *I* formation is symbolized in dreams by a fortified camp, or even a stadium – distributing, between the arena within its walls and its outer border of gravel-pits and marshes' (2006a: 78). Here we are approaching an understanding of Lacan's conception of the subject. Through the mirror stage, the subject deceives itself into coherence through a phantasmic relation to the other. The subject misrecognises a coherence that represses its fragmented character. Hence, for Lacan: 'The subject is no one. It is decomposed, in pieces. And it is jammed, sucked in by the image, the deceiving and realised image, of the other, or equally by its own specular image. That is where it finds its unity' (1988: 54).

As Lacan's teaching continued, we find this notion of the 'decentrement' of the subject elaborated and extended. A decisive shift is signalled by the introduction of the category of 'the Real', a concept which becomes increasingly important for Lacan and which, as we saw earlier, is central to Laclau and Mouffe's conception of society, which is variously taken up and then forgotten by du Gay and Fournier and Grey. Refusing to see Lacan as an idealist (see Lacan, 1979: 53), or seeing symbolisation as total, Lacan identifies the Real as that which escapes symbolisation.

In order to clarify what is meant by the Lacanian Real and its role in signification and subjectification, consider the famous but puzzling painting by Hans Holbein, *The Ambassadors* (see Lacan, 1979: 88–89). In this painting we find two subjects who appear before us constructed and hailed by the signs around them. Their fine clothes indicate their wealth, the oriental rug indicates that these are men of travel and experience, and the instruments of the arts and sciences of the time indicate that these are learned renaissance men. It appears that we have a relatively successful interpellation – the figures are hailed by the signifiers that surround them, and they answer with a definite identity of being ambassadors, the painting's simplistic title. However there is an obstacle in interpreting the image in this way, and this obstacle, which will be faced by any merely interpretive approach to the problem, comes in the form of a strange shape at the feet of the ambassadors. Is this a silly mistake by one of Holbein's scoundrel apprentices? Is it the pelt of an animal worn by 'howling savages' from a far-off land? If the viewer inspects this shape from the correct angle, they are struck by a skull staring them right in the face. All the fineries of life-affirming wealth suddenly pale into insignificance as this horrific reminder of death opens a hole in the signifying chain. It is this hole which then comes to frame, shape, and indeed 'motivate' the pattern of signification. The two men are not only interpellated as ambassadors (men of learning, experience, and wealth), but are also simultaneously 'pulled apart' by the ghost of mortality indicated by the skull. This skull points us towards the Lacanian Real – the traumatic, unspeakable of death in this case. Moreover, it is this 'silent' Real of death (whose place is held by the traumatic signifier of the skull) which throws the rest of the signification in the painting into being as signifiers. The Real, this rupture in the symbolic fabric, is 'the stroke of the opening that makes absence emerge – just as the cry does not stand out against a background of silence, but on the contrary makes the silence emerge as silence' (Lacan, 1979: 26).

LACK IS IN THE OTHER

The Real appears, then, as an obstacle to the effective constitution of the subject in discourse, and, for us, is one of the markers which distinguishes Lacan from Foucault. Having identified a lack in the subject, which the subject attempts to stitch up or 'suture' through its Imaginary relation to the other (see Miller, 1978), the Real produces a limit or lack in the Symbolic order or, to put it simply, a lack in the other. Hence, we have moved some distance from the simplistic 'mirror stage' image of the subject recognising itself in the other, to finding the subject lacking or 'barred' in relation to the other. By corollary, when a subject recognises itself in the 'mirror' of discourse (subsequently constructing their subjectivity) they never achieve full recognition. The subject never closes on the centre of the subjectivity which is imputed in discourse because the subject is structured around a traumatic central gap – which is what Lacan calls 'the Real'. The subject is never able to fully internalise and identify with the other of discourse. There is something in the subject that resists, or more accurately 'escapes' vocalisation.

For Lacan, it is this inability to close on the gap within ourselves, to 'truly become ourselves' that keeps us becoming, identifying and speaking. It is this central gap in identification from which our (impossible) desire to identify flows. We speak because we cannot quite explain ourselves, because our explanation of ourselves is lacking. If we closed this gap in our identity (an event which would be impossible, for Lacan), then the business of constant chatter about who we are, what we want, how we plan to get it and so on, would come to an end. It is that which is 'in the subject more than the subject' that makes us subjects and keeps us subjected (Lacan, 1979: ch. 20).

So not only is the subject barred by a central traumatic gap, the other with which the subject attempts to identify is also barred. Hence the Lacanian formula 'the big other does not exist', and the crossing out not simply of the subject but more radically of the other. Not only is the subject structured around an unsignifiable lack, the other with which the subject identifies is also structured around a central lack. After the subject searches for something in themselves which they can identify with and fails, it turns towards the other. This search for the other is bound to fail, just as an attempt to answer 'who is God?', or 'what is Virtue?' proves ultimately futile. Each of these attempts to answer who or what the big other is ultimately finds itself wallowing in futile attempts to fill in an unsignifiable universal with particulars. Repeated attempts to identify who or what this big other is seems to only uncover a gap in signification – something we cannot say.

It is this central gap, the traumatic kernel, the unsignifiable lack in the other that motivates and drives our attempts to keep on identifying with it. Even though the other demands something from us – discourse about God demands devotion, discourse about virtue, virtuosity – the demand of the other is both impossible and yet prohibited. The fact that we can never completely subsume the other, that we can never fully incorporate it into our language, drives our attempts to identify with it, and our attempts to speak it. It is the unrepresentable nature of God which has kept religious iconologists and priests in work for thousands of years, and it is the unrepresentable nature of virtue which keeps Euthyphro and Meno attempting to explain what virtue is to Socrates. It is this gap in the other which provides the subject with 'breathing space'. The subject not only experiences lack in themselves, but lack in the other. It is this lack in the other which motivates our consistent attempt (despite, or precisely *because of* our continual failure) to internalise the other.

THE SEARCH FOR THE HEFFALUMP

Having briefly outlined Lacanian concepts of the subject and the Real, let us now return to the question of the enterprise. We can find examples of Lacanian concepts such as lack in the other in the most unexpected places, and this is clearly visible in the variety of scientific and pseudo-scientific research that has been devoted to the search for the entrepreneur. In such studies the most detailed researches have been conducted into establishing once and for all the character of the entrepreneur, asking what exactly it is that makes an entrepreneur an entrepreneur. A raft of propositions about the positive identity of the entrepreneur has appeared, including need for achievement (McClelland, 1961; Johnson, 1990), internal locus of control (Duchesneau and Gartner, 1990), low-risk aversion (van Praag and Cramer, 2001), and self-reliance and extraversion (Lee and Tsang, 2001).

But right from the beginnings of this now well-established research programme, the entrepreneur has not yielded to empirical analysis. Researchers seem to continually run into failure. For example, one writer complains: 'for ten years we ran a research centre in entrepreneurial history, for ten years we tried to define the entrepreneur. We never succeeded' (Cole, 1969: 17). Some use more colourful and romantic language to describe their failure:

> The search for the source of dynamic entrepreneurial performance has much in common with hunting the Heffalump. The Heffalump is a rather large and very important animal [see Milne, 1926, 1928]. He has been hunted by many individuals using various ingenious trapping devices, but no one so far has succeeded

in capturing him. All who claim to have caught sight of him report that he is enormous, but they disagree on his particularities. Not having explored his current habitat with sufficient care, some hunters have used as bait their own favorite dishes and have tried to persuade people that what they caught was a Heffalump. However very few are convinced, and the search goes on. (Kilby, 1971: 1)

Such a pattern of failure is not part of the distant past of entrepreneurship research, as it seems quite clear that there has been little reward for the increased research effort over the last forty years. Contemporary proponents of entrepreneurship repeat the woeful refrain of their predecessors: ' there is no generic definition of the entrepreneur' (Brockhaus and Horwitz, 1986: 42), 'entrepreneurship is like obscenity: Nobody agrees what it is, but we all know it when we see it' (Shaver and Scott, 1991: 24), 'There is little empirical evidence to support the notion that a single trait or collection of traits can explain the business behaviour of many widely different entrepreneurs' (Grey, 1998: 151). Hence, after all these years, proponents of entrepreneurship remain dismayed that 'the study of entrepreneurship is still in its infancy' (Brazeal and Herbert, 1999: 29).

All of these authors see this 'litany of errors' as an indication of the correctable failure of entrepreneurship research. The failure of all past efforts only hardens their resolve and indicates that they simply need to try harder. Hence the failure of all previous research into the character of the entrepreneur is taken to be something to do with the failings of earlier researchers ('they didn't try hard enough, they didn't apply the right method . . .'), rather than something to do with the object of enquiry.

The failure to find the centre of entrepreneurship in the subject of the entrepreneur has led some entrepreneurship researchers towards investigations of 'structural' factors outside the subjectivity of the entrepreneur. These include experiential factors such as individual entrepreneur's prior experience and education which allows them to recognise opportunities and innovate (Shane, 2000); firm-level factors such as organisation context, firm resources and competitive strategy (Entrialgo et al., 2001); inter-organizational factors including networking activities such as firm and number of partners (Lee and Tsang, 2001); an existing community of entrepreneurs, especially in new industry creation (Mezias and Kuperman, 2001); the industry population density (Manigrat, 1994); industry structure (Herron and Robinson, 1993); societal level factors including national culture (Thomas and Mueller, 2000; Mueller and Thomas, 2001); and state entrepreneurial climate, particularly availability of financial capital for entrepreneurs (Goetz and Freshwater, 2001).

The proliferation of structural causes has led entrepreneurship researchers to suggest that the 'traumatic kernel' of chaotic penetrations of a variety of causal factors may be the cause of the entrepreneur (Bygrave, 1989a, 1989b; Smilor and Feeser, 1991). It therefore appears that the central gap of chance which brings a variety of causal factors together lies at the centre of the other of enterprise discourse. Indeed Ogbor's (2000) and Armstrong's (2005) critical analyses of the ideology of entrepreneurship argue that *the* defining feature of entrepreneurship discourse is the consistent and congenital failure to positively identify the entrepreneur. All entrepreneurship research therefore can offer us is a continued failure to find the character of the entrepreneur and a massive proliferation of 'other' structural determinants of entrepreneurship.

SUCCESS IN FAILURE

But what if research into the entrepreneur has, in its very failure, identified something critically important about the operation of the category of the entrepreneur, that it is essentially indefinable, vacuous and empty? What if entrepreneurship research has not failed at all, but has uncovered something significant about the underlying structure of entrepreneurship discourse, that is, that 'the entrepreneur' is an empty signifier, an open space or 'lack' whose operative function is not to 'exist' in the usual sense but to structure phantasmic attachment? This would be the Lacanian hypothesis – that the entrepreneur is a marker of this lack, the entrepreneur is indefinable and necessarily so, the entrepreneur is an 'absent centre'. To say all of this is to make a decisive shift in the way that we think about objects, introducing as it does the order of a quite different thing, not the thing that we commonly perceive but what Žižek calls a 'sublime object'.

When we speak of the 'failure' of entrepreneurship research, then, we are not talking of failure in the normal sense. We are thinking of a logic of 'failure' which, in its very act of repetition, brings to light a deeper and more profound truth. This could be thought of as failure in the Hegelian sense, in the way that the course of 'errors' of the past brings to light a higher order of truth. This logic is revealed clearly in a number of what Žižek calls 'Hegelian jokes' (Žižek, 1989: 64–6, 160–61, 173–8). For example, Žižek tells the joke of a conscript who tries to avoid military service by pretending to be mad.

> His symptom is that he compulsively checks all the pieces of paper he can lay his hands on, constantly repeating: 'That is not it!'. He is sent to the military psychiatrist, in whose office he also examines all the papers around, including those in the wastepaper basket, repeating all the time: 'That is not it!'. The psychiatrist, finally convinced that he really is mad, gives him a written warrant

releasing him from military service. The conscript casts a look at it and says cheerfully 'That *is* it!'. (Žižek, 1989: 160)

The point is that a certain truth comes to light by the repetition of failure. As Žižek explains, 'The "mad" conscript pretends to look for something, and through his very search, through its repeated failure ("That is not it!"), he produces what he is looking for' (Žižek, 1989: 160). We could suggest that we have much the same situation with entrepreneurship research. The search for the character of the entrepreneur and for the structural factors which cause entrepreneurship continually fail.

While this is generally not treated as a failure, indicating the need to try harder, the Lacanian insight is that this failure is indicative of the deep structure of the operation of the object of the entrepreneurship. Rather than flummoxing around cursing and say 'That is not it! That is not it!', entrepreneurship research has discovered something very important which should not be denied but interrogated. Following Lacan, that *is* it! We should stress that failure takes place at *both* the level of the subject and at the level of the structure. This makes us suspicious, therefore, of any notion of 'structuration' (see, for example, Sarason et al., 2006), which would promise a tidy victory but would run the risk of resulting in a 'double failure' by failing to account for the impossibility of both the subject and structure.

In line with the unmasking we seek to perform here, there is something peculiar about enterprise and entrepreneurship which is generally denied. What is denied is something central about the very object of the entrepreneur, something which, we have argued, is glimpsed by entrepreneurship research, but is rationalised and hence pushed out of sight. We are suggesting that entrepreneurship is not a coherent and stable discourse which is held together around a stable centre. Such a unity is almost always assumed by functionalist approaches to entrepreneurship, and this is something a critical perspective brings to light. Rather, it is a paradoxical, incomplete and worm-ridden symbolic structure which posits an impossible and indeed incomprehensible object at its centre. To put it in the strictest Lacanian formulation, entrepreneurship discourse does not exist.

In a quite different sense, of course, entrepreneurship discourse clearly does exist. It offers a narrative structure to the fantasy which coordinates desire. It points to an unattainable and only vaguely specified object, and directs desire towards that object. And here the Lacanian formula 'What desire desires is desire itself' is particularly useful. It is not in 'being' an entrepreneur that one secures identity, but in the gap between the subject and the object of desire. Not only does it not matter that the object is unattainable, but this lack is central to maintaining desiring. And as Lacan indicates, if we ever achieve the object of desire it collapses, it falls apart and is changed inexplicably into a gift of shit. We find that Bill Gates is just an ordinary human being, wrought with his perfectly normal and human neuroticism, but is elevated to heroic status as if there is something unique to his psyche which is the ultimate cause of his economic successes. It is precisely the paradoxical and apparently mysterious nature of entrepreneurship discourse that allows it to be such a continually effective discourse in enlisting budding entrepreneurs, and reproducing political and economic relations. It is these political and economic relations to which we will now turn.

4. The birth of the entrepreneur

One of the remarkable things missing in both functionalist and interpretive accounts is the political and economic consequences of entrepreneurship. Although interpretive research has tried to open up the concept, what tends to disappear is the notion that the entrepreneur is an economic category. The danger with expanding the entrepreneur into all areas of social life (see for example Steyaert and Hjorth, 2006) has been to lose sight of the political and economic nature of entrepreneurship. As Murtola (2008) notes, these 'dirty' aspects of entrepreneurship are effectively denied, and in doing so, entrepreneurship, as she puts it, is 'redeemed'. In this chapter, far from redeeming entrepreneurship or allowing it to escape its economic consequences, we propose to engage with the task of what might be called historical political economy.

Instead of seeing enterprise as a magic cure to the problems of late modernity, critics see talk of entrepreneurship as politically charged. A central lesson from the critique of entrepreneurship is that the consistent attribution of positive value to entrepreneurship simultaneously marginalises other economic actors. When positive value is bestowed upon the notion of the entrepreneur, it becomes the locus of virtues as wide-ranging as efficiency, innovation, self-fulfilment and response to consumer demand, and, as it was put long ago 'intelligence, prudence, probity and regularity' (Say, 1821: 330). These positive valuations stand in notable contrast to the apparent ills of bureaucracy such as inefficiency, routinisation, responsiveness to rules, self-depreciation and a workplace thoroughly disenchanted by instrumental rationality.

Critics of entrepreneurship have provided powerful descriptions of how today we value entrepreneurship positively. But when and how did this positive valuation of the entrepreneur emerge? In this chapter we offer tentative answers to this question by outlining a genealogy of the valuation of the entrepreneur. We first indicate what we mean by a genealogy of value, and then describe a set of historical shifts in the valuation of different economic characters, paying particular attention to the emergence of the entrepreneur as claimant on value. We use this historical sketch as the basis for a discussion of the broader question of the politics of the valuation of the entrepreneur in relation to other economic actors.

FOR A GENEALOGY OF VALUE

In order to understand how the entrepreneur is ascribed value, we need to look at the processes of valuation. One of the difficulties with this is that valuation is multifaceted. That is, by claiming that an economic actor like the entrepreneur is valuable, we are connecting a number of wildly different, but subtly interlinked types of value. The major dynamic of valuation that is recognized by critics such as du Gay (1996) is that enterprise culture ascribes a positive *cultural* value to the entrepreneur. This means that the entrepreneur and all of the things this figure is supposed to represent becomes a kind of revered 'master signifier' in a given culture that might stand alongside democracy and freedom. Another dynamic of valuation involved with enterprise culture is the ascription of a *moral* value to the entrepreneur. By this we mean that the ethos or way of life that the entrepreneur is supposed to embody comes to represent a kind of exemplar of the good life. Bound up with the cultural and moral valuation processes of enterprise culture is a third process that inscribes an *economic* value to the entrepreneur. This works not only by positively valuing the cultural and moral traits of the entrepreneur, but by assigning a cold cash value to what the entrepreneur brings to the process of production. Although critics of entrepreneurship have largely shied away from the third set of questions, in this chapter, we want to stress the way that the valuation of the entrepreneur is not merely a cultural or moral affair, but is also a matter of political economy.

We also encounter questions of how to think about valuation. Often people treat value as if it contains an essence. This happens when an object is said to contain within it a particular value that only needs to be identified through schooled investigation. An example would be the claim that gold, or Proust's *In Search of Lost Time* is in itself 'valuable'. The problem with this way of approaching value is that we find wild shifts in valuation over time. Put simply: we value different things, and value things differently at different points in time. For this reason, many have been led to see value and valuation as *contingent* affairs. Possibly the most famous amongst those stressing the contingency of value is Friedrich Nietzsche, who highlighted the variability of values which are held dear in modern culture. Nietzsche set himself the goal of uncovering the ignoble origins of 'noble' things such as what we call 'morality' and, in the process, recommends a 'transvaluation' of our present values (Nietzsche, 1968). Nietzsche therefore proposed a genealogy of our values, which would not be to relativise all values, but to show how we could value things differently. Through an historical excavation of the vagaries of valuation Nietzsche argued that 'we need a critique of all moral values;

the intrinsic worth of these values must, first of all, be called into question' (Nietzsche, 1956: 155). Nietzsche's transvaluation of values inspired
Foucault's genealogical study of the emergence of modern economics.
In part of a broader study of the human sciences, Foucault drew on an
archive of economic texts that shows a profound shift in how the economy
is described. In particular Foucault (1970: chs. 6 and 8) charted a shift
from studies of the circulation of wealth through to modern economics,
and with this shift the invention of basic concepts that are now taken for
granted in economic thought.

One prominent contemporary proponent of a contingency approach
to value is Barbara Herrnstein Smith, who argues for what she calls an
anti-essentialist understanding of value (Smith, 1988; see also Andrew,
1995; Shapiro, 1993). Discussing the valuation of literature, she examines
the common assumption amongst literary critics that there are particular works of art or literature, such as Shakespeare's sonnets, which are
of absolute value. These works are often attributed value because of
the 'inherent qualities of certain objects and/or some presumed human
universals' (Smith, 1988: 36). In contrast with the argument that value is
something which is absolute and all those who do not recognize this can be
accused of mental deficiency, Smith proposes that value is the product of a
continued process of cultural circulation. Valuations are not 'discrete acts
or episodes punctuating experience' (Smith, 1988: 42) where the value of a
given object is calculated once and for all. Rather, valuation is conceived
as 'indistinguishable from the very process of acting and experiencing the
self' (Smith, 1988: 42). This process of experience however is not one which
begins afresh, but which involves the encounter of pre-marked signs:

> We do not, however, move about in a raw universe. Not only are the objects we
> encounter always to some extent pre-interpreted and pre-classified for us by our
> cultures and languages; they are also pre-evaluated, bearing marks and signs of
> their prior valuings and evaluations by our fellow creatures. (Smith, 1988: 42)

The value that is ascribed to a given object in our continuing processes of
valuation is therefore contingent upon various pre-evaluations. Following
this, value is 'neither a fixed attribute, an inherent quality, or an objective
property of things but, rather, an effect of multiple, continuously changing, and continuously interacting variables' (Smith, 1988: 30). Studying
how something comes to be valued involves not looking into the particular
subject at hand and attempting to establish its true value, but investigating
the 'pre-evaluations' and 're-evaluations' which are made of the object by
various parties. Investigating the valuation of entrepreneurship, we are
not asking how intrinsically valuable entrepreneurship is, but rather how

entrepreneurship has been valued, and how this valuation might be critically rethought.

Our analysis of the value of the entrepreneur would therefore begin by asking what values are apportioned to different economic categories at different points in time. It would also ask how economic categories suddenly come to be valued. In this process of the contingent valuation of various categories, we investigate the struggle which occurs between different codes of valuation. It is these changing valuations of economic categories, and the 'birth' of the entrepreneur, that we will consider in this chapter.

Before turning to history we should also note that questions of valuation are fundamentally intertwined with questions of distribution (Fraser, 1997; Fraser and Honneth, 2003). This is to say that if something is judged to be valuable, then notions of equity will lead us to distribute rewards in favour of that thing. So for instance, if we value the paintings of Picasso, then we are more likely to pay more in return for one of his works than for the works of other artists. From this, three claims about value can be advanced. First, value is contingent, that is, different things are valued at different points in time. Second, value is a relational phenomenon, that is, if one thing is judged more valuable then others are judged less valuable. Third, judgements of value also imply judgements of just reward, that is, the attribution of value and the distribution of wealth are two sides of the same coin.

In order to unmask the pre-history of value that lurks behind contemporary accounts of the entrepreneur we will therefore look at how value has been apportioned in the economic literature. Because there are already extensive treatises in the history of economic thought, our goal is not to produce a comprehensive history of the entrepreneur in economic thought. Rather, we shall pursue a less ambitious survey of some of the well-known metamorphoses in conceptions of value from mercantilism and physiocracy through Smith and Ricardo to the 'discovery' of the entrepreneur by Schumpeter and others in the early years of the twentieth century. This survey will then provide us with a point from which to launch a more detailed discussion of the politics of valuing the entrepreneur.

FROM LAND AND LABOUR TO THE TRINITY FORMULA

Writing principally in the second half of the eighteenth century, the physiocrats signify a point of departure from what Smith called mercantilism. The mercantilists, a loose collection of traders and advisers to state, continued the ancient conception of international rivalry for wealth, according to which the goal of the state is to amass wealth, which comes in the form of recognised coinage – gold or silver, for example. Between nations exists a perpetual contest for such wealth. In times of peace this contest takes place through foreign trade, and the goal of this should always be, in the classic yet still recognisable formula, 'to sell more to strangers yearly than we consume of theirs in value' (Mun, 1664: ch. 2).

While the mercantilists envisioned a zero-sum game with foreign trade as the ultimate strategy for competitive victory, the physiocrats viewed wealth as a result of internal commerce, and most importantly of agriculture. In their conception of the value of agriculture we confront the most controversial of physiocratic doctrines. The physiocrats began from the now-commonsensical proposition that any productive undertaking requires an initial outgoing, which is then offset against any wealth produced. The excess of new wealth against the cost of outgoings they called the 'net product'. But controversially, the physiocrats claimed that this net product was solely the result of one form of production, that is, agricultural production. Hence Quesnay (1759) distinguishes between three classes, a 'productive class' consisting of agriculturalists, a 'proprietary class' consisting of land owners and aristocrats and a 'sterile class' consisting of traders, manufacturers and domestic servants. Of these it is only agricultural workers that are 'productive', in the sense that only they produce a net product greater than their cost of subsistence. Those working in industry are 'sterile' insofar as they simply modify the net product of the land. The proprietary class lives on the activity of both the others on the basis that they are the owners of land.

In terms of claims about value we can see how, on one reading, the physiocrats find land to be the sole source of all value. But we cannot simply assume that the physiocrats treat land as the sole source of value, because of the presence of the category of 'productive labour'. Even if it is restricted to a specific type of labour, it is nonetheless not simply land but also *labour* on land that produces value. Here we are not too far away then from the duality of value that we find in Petty and Cantillon. For Petty, 'Labour is the Father and active principle of Wealth, as Lands are the Mother' (Petty, 1662: 68). For Cantillon, 'Land is the source or matter from which we draw wealth; the labour of man is the form that produces it' (Cantillon, 1755: ch. 1, see also ch.10). To simplify, we could codify these sources of twin value and their respective rewards into the schema in Figure 4.1.

Even if the idea that value is the result of a duality of land and labour held sway in physiocratic (and other) circles in the seventeenth and eighteenth centuries, this was rarely uncontested, and more importantly the consequences of this duality were never agreed upon. If land and labour are the two sources of value then what is the consequence? Petty tried to find ways

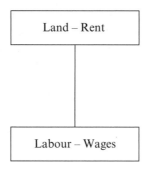

Figure 4.1   Land and labour as sources of value

in which the two could be 'balanced'. The physiocrats, according to some, provided an ideological justification for the aristocracy by privileging land over labour. Alternatively, someone such as Turgot, working at the limits of physiocracy, suggests that because those who work on the land are the only ones whose labour produces anything over the cost of their labour, labour is 'therefore the sole source of all wealth' (Turgot, 1774: ch. 7).

Towards the end of the eighteenth century we move away from a duality of land and labour following the introduction of capital as a third source of value, hence what Marx calls the 'trinity formula': capital–interest, land–ground rent, labour–wages (1894: 814; see Figure 4.2). This trinity is perfectly formalised by Mill, for whom the requisites of production 'may be reduced to three: labour, capital, and the materials and motive forces afforded by nature' (Mill, 1848: 63). Ricardo also writes:

> The produce of the earth – all that is derived from its surface by the united application of labour, machinery and capital, is divided among three classes of the community, namely, the proprietor of the land, the owner of the stock or capital necessary for its cultivation, and the labourers by whose industry it is cultivated. (Ricardo, 1817: 3)

But once again, the crucially important thing is how these three sources of value are valued. Mill, for example, argues that these three sources are not of equal value, concluding that 'labour and the raw material of the globe are primary and indispensable' (Mill, 1848: 63). The reason for this is that 'capital is itself the product of labour: its instrumentality in production is therefore, in reality, that of labour in indirect shape' (Mill, 1848: 63). But while Mill reintroduces the duality of land and labour by disqualifying the distinct status of capital as a source of value, we find a conflict between those who advance a trinity and those who reduce value back to a single source. Notable here are proponents of a labour theory of value, who

insist that land and capital are imposters, both making false claims on
the products of labour. Marx, for example, dismisses that trinity formula,
objecting that land, labour and capital 'belong to widely dissimilar spheres
and are not at all analogous with one another. They have about the same
relation to each other as lawyer's fees, red beets and music' (Marx, 1894:
814). Offering an argument that bears striking analogies to what we saw in
Turgot, Marx asks how anything other than the products of human labour
can be attributed with value, and finds appeals to the self-valorising character of capital to be a shabby case of self-interested presumption.

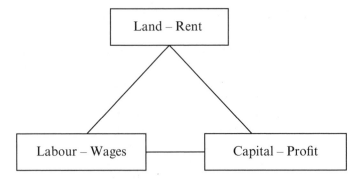

Figure 4.2   The trinity formula

So at the same time that the trinity formula begins to establish itself
and is taken as self-evident by many, we also find objections and counter-
arguments. Rather than becoming an established economic doctrine in the
nineteenth century the trinity formula is asserted, but never quite stabilises.
Then at the end of the nineteenth century and the beginning of the twentieth century, we find a new form of contestation, and a strange bifurcation
in economic discourse. On the one hand we find the rise of marginalism
and the birth of an 'economic science' that has no truck with discussions
of value. On the other hand, we find the trinity reinvented, but now with a
new figure standing proudly alongside land, labour and capital.

BEYOND THE TRINITY FORMULA

In the early twentieth century the trinity formula is irrevocably disturbed
when an old character puts forward a new value claim. Schumpeter begins
The Theory of Economic Development with an analysis of the economic
cycle, arguing that the combination of the familiar factors of production

– land, labour, and capital – tends toward a state of equilibrium. As this equilibrium is approached the rewards for land, labour, and capital diminish. Schumpeter cautions us not to go looking for extra-economic factors such as wars, religion, or politics to explain 'spontaneous and discontinuous changes' in the economy. Rather, 'changes in economic life are not forced upon it from without, but arise by its own initiative, from within' (Schumpeter, 1934: 63). Further, Schumpeter does not locate the drivers of economic development in land, labour or capital but rather in a figure who carries out new combinations of these productive factors. 'The carrying out of new combinations we call "enterprise"; the individuals whose function it is to carry them out we call "entrepreneurs"' (1934: 74). Here we have the emergence of the fourth point that definitively disrupts the trinity formula, giving birth to a new source of value – by rediscovering the 'adventurer' that Say (1821) evoked a century before, and now consistently calling this character 'the entrepreneur'. The trinity of land, labour and capital becomes a quadrangle of land, labour, capital and entrepreneurship (see Figure 4.3).

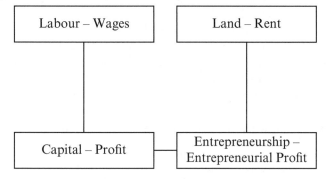

Figure 4.3   The entrepreneur as source of value

With the emergence of this fourth character in the economic drama, a fourth claim on value is advanced, for what Schumpeter calls 'entrepreneurial profit'. Schumpeter is clear that this claim is in addition to any other claims – simply called 'costs' – made by labour in the form of a wage, land in the form of rent, or capital in the form of interest. Hence:

> Entrepreneurial profit is a surplus over costs. From the standpoint of the entrepreneur, it is the difference between receipts and outlay in a business, as we have already been told by a long line of economists. Superficial as this definition is, it is sufficient as a starting point. By 'outlay' we understand all the disbursements which the entrepreneur must make directly or indirectly in production. To this must be added an appropriate wage for labour performed by the entrepreneur,

an appropriate rent for any land which may chance to belong to him, and
finally a premium for risk. (Schumpeter, 1934: 128)

After recognising the additional value that might be created by economic
development, the reader may be tempted to wonder just who is it that
'adventures' such economic changes. Who is it that consequently should
be rewarded for such developments? Perhaps the reckless reader may
begin to recall the description of the under-aged 'entrepreneur' toiling
in Adam Smith's pin factory. Perhaps the reader may take managerial
discourses like Total Quality Management seriously and assume that it is
the worker on the shop floor who is the source of innovation. Perhaps the
reader may even begin to believe that the inventor of a new technology
may have some value claim. But before the reader is allowed to be deluded
in these ways, Schumpeter assures us that it is only in the process of bring-
ing these new combinations together that this new claim on value resides.
Schumpeter asks to whom this surplus created by enterprise falls, and
answers: 'Obviously to the individual who introduces the loom into the
circular flow, not to the mere inventors, but also not to the mere producers
or users of them' (1934: 132).

So the apparently inert factors like labour or technical innovation that
are brought together by the entrepreneur have no special claim on value.
This assertion that the entrepreneur has a legitimate value claim obviously
begs the question of what these individuals under consideration have con-
tributed to production, but Schumpeter is quick to allay our fears:

> Only the will and the action, not the concrete goods; for they have bought
> these – either from others or from themselves; not the purchasing power with
> which they bought, for they borrowed this – from others or, if we take account
> of acquisition in earlier periods, from themselves. And what have they done?
> They have not accumulated any kind of goods, they have created no original
> means of production, but they employed existing means of production differ-
> ently, more appropriately, more advantageously. They have 'carried out new
> combinations'. They are entrepreneurs. And their profit, the surplus, to which
> no liability corresponds, is an entrepreneurial profit. (Schumpeter, 1934: 132)

Schumpeter understands how little the entrepreneur might actually bring
to the party, not having had to endure the toil of labour, the risk of losing
capital, or the inconvenience of allowing production to take place on one's
land. No liability corresponds to the entrepreneur except the idea of 'lead-
ership' in combining the factors of production. Schumpeter appears to be
quite aware of the possibility of disputing the value claim of the entrepreneur, and is also aware that the entrepreneur is not a new face in the neigh-
bourhood of economic theory. The entrepreneur appears in Cantillon in

his claim that the entrepreneur is a character who buys goods at a certain price and sells them at an uncertain price. But for Cantillon (1755) the entrepreneur is indistinguishable from the petty capitalist trader who is at the centre of mercantilist theory. The entrepreneur also appears in the economics of Say (1821), who introduces the entrepreneur in distinguishing interest on capital from profit. For Say, the entrepreneur is inseparable from the capitalist who is at the centre of classical economics.

The entrepreneur also makes an appearance in the writing of contemporaries of Schumpeter, notably in the marginalist economics of Alfred Marshall. In his *Principles of Economics* Marshall identifies the entrepreneurial function with the activity of the business manager. He argues that on top of outlays such as materials, rent, wages and interest for capital must be added 'the earnings of undertaking or management' (1890: 2, iv, 2). Rather less boldly than Schumpeter, and claiming that 'the earnings of the undertaker' constitute a legitimate claim on value, Marshall argues that 'labour together with capital and land thus defined are the sources of all that income of which account is commonly taken in reckoning up the National Income' (1890: 2, iv, 6). Given three principle sources of value for Marshall, where do the earnings of the undertaker fall? The joint stock company is evoked as an instructive example:

> In them [joint stock companies] most of the work of management is divided between salaried directors (who indeed hold a few shares themselves) and salaried managers and other subordinate officials, most of whom have little or no capital of any kind; and their earnings, being almost the pure earnings of labour, are governed in the long run by those general causes which rule the earnings of labour of equal difficulty and disagreeableness in ordinary occupations. (Marshall, 1890: 6, vii, 6)

For Marshall, the earnings of management or the undertaker are a *special kind of wage* (1890: 6, viii). Marshall's 'earnings of management' are an instructive counterpoint to Schumpeter's 'entrepreneurial profit'. The most obvious reason for this is that both appear to posit almost exactly the same form in reckoning the earnings of management or entrepreneurial profit (incomes less receipts, which include rent, wages, and interest). While Schumpeter sees the entrepreneur as presenting an extra value claim, Marshall sees the *manager* as entitled to a special kind of wage. As is well documented, this is exactly the historical moment at which entrepreneurial capitalism is being replaced with monopoly capitalism and modern bureaucratic management (Baran and Sweezy, 1966; Bendix, 1956; Chandler, 1977). What is interesting here is that at almost the precise historical point of this transition, we find Schumpeter suddenly 'discovering' the entrepreneur, while Marshall is speaking of the value of management.

It could also be argued that Frank Knight's *Risk, Uncertainty and Profit* provides a bridge between Marshall's awareness of the growth of monopoly capitalism, and Schumpeter's fantasies about a fading world of small-time 'undertakers'. Knight argues that the role of the entrepreneur is not to engage in 'mere activity' but to manage the uncertainty thrown up by economic and social life: 'With uncertainty present, doing things, the actual execution of activity, becomes in a real sense a secondary part of life; the primary problem or function is deciding what to do and how to do it' (1921: 268). But unlike Schumpeter, Knight is under no illusions that the entrepreneurial function is carried out by the lone entrepreneur. Instead, managing uncertainty is rapidly ceded to bureaucratic managers:

> When uncertainty is present and the task of deciding what to do and how to do it takes the ascendancy over that execution, the internal organization of the productive groups is no longer a matter of indifference or a mechanical detail. Centralization of this deciding and controlling function is imperative. (Knight, 1921: 268)

For Knight the figure of the 'entrepreneur' in large bureaucratic organisations 'may, and typically will, to be sure, continue to perform the old mechanical routine functions and receive the old wages; but in addition he makes responsible decisions, and his income will normally contain in addition to wages a pure *differential* element designated as "profit" by the economic theorists' (Knight, 1921: 276–7). Knight goes on to specify that 'this profit is simply the difference between the market price of the productive agencies he employs' such as land, labour and capital, which are given a valuation by 'the amount which the competition of other entrepreneurs forces him to guarantee to them' and 'the amount which he finally realizes from the disposition of the product which under his direction they turn out' (1921: 277). The upshot of this is that Knight's entrepreneur/ manager carries out a peculiar two-fold function of (1) exercising responsible control for which a wage is rewarded, and (2) protecting the owners of productive services against uncertainty and fluctuation in their income for which entrepreneurial profit is rewarded. In short, the bureaucratic manager, not the capitalist, has two claims on value.

So while the twentieth century brings to light a fourth claimant on value, between Schumpeter, Marshall and Knight we find agreement that this fourth value claim needs to be advanced. But simultaneously there is a disagreement as to who it is that will be entitled to make this fourth claim. For Schumpeter, it falls largely to the innovative, relatively independent capitalist, but for Marshall and Knight it is the manager. Perhaps we should not be too surprised when we see economists today disagreeing about the sources of the productivity of the economy, even if they agree that it must be attributed to a fourth, and systematically mysterious, character.

CONSEQUENCES

This rough outline of historical shifts in valuation highlights remarkable variation in the value awarded to various economic actors. We see that there is a whole history of economic discourse that underlies the apparently practical act of apportioning value to an economic actor like the entrepreneur. In physiocratic doctrine, economic value was located in the factors of land represented by the landowner and labour represented by the peasantry. Because they produce value, these two economic actors are able to put forward value claims with the landowner claiming rent, and the peasant claiming what we would now call a wage. In the late eighteenth century a third figure appears on the economic stage and puts forward a further claim on value. This is the figure of the capitalist who claims to contribute to the production of value through venturing capital and thereby risking an uncertain return. In exchange for risking capital, the capitalist makes a third value claim in the form of interest. This trinity of land, labour and capital is once again disturbed with the appearance of a fourth actor on the economic stage. Economic discourses now insist that entrepreneurs also add value by combining the other factors of production in a novel fashion. For this essential service they put forward yet another claim on value in the form of entrepreneurial profit. We therefore arrive at the present-day quadrangle of economic actors and associated rewards: land-rent, labour-wages, capital-interest, and entrepreneur-entrepreneurial profit.

One general lesson we can draw from the history of the valuation of the entrepreneur is that economics does not simply describe the reality of value-production but is actively implicated in the act of sharing out the value that is rewarded to each actor. Such a recognition stands in dramatic contrast to discussions of value by economists who generally search for the ultimate bedrock, the 'essence' of value. We often find claims that the source of value 'really' is land by the physiocrats, or 'really' is labour according to the labour theory of value. Equally, with representatives of the trinity formula we find suggestions that value is an entity to be discovered, and that it might be discovered alongside other natural economic laws. Hence the 'essentialism' of Ricardo who argues that:

> in different stages of society, the proportions of the whole produce of the earth which will be allocated to each of these classes [land, capital and labour], under the names of rent, profit and wages, will be essentially different; depending

mainly on the actual fertility of the soil, on the accumulation of capital and population, and on the skill, ingenuity, and instruments employed in agriculture. To determine *the laws which regulate this distribution* is the principal problem of political economy (Ricardo, 1817: 3, emphasis added).

As usual, we find this essentialism in extreme form in Mill, for whom 'the laws and conditions of the production of wealth, partake of the character of physical truths. There is nothing optional, or arbitrary in them' (Mill, 1848: 122). We wonder if this situation is much better with Schumpeter or with contemporary talk about entrepreneurship. Here we find the assertion, or rather the assumption, that the valuation of the factors of production is a matter of fact, rather than a matter of value, which is ironic, given that these essentialists of value tend to each value the factors differently.

Against this, our outline of a genealogy of the valuation of the entrepreneur finds an historical multiplication of the sources of value. Moreover, we have also uncovered the fact that there is significant tension and contestation involved within each of the epochs that we have described. Even the apparently simple physiocratic claim that value resides in land and labour is already internally split between two claimants. What we mean by this is that even with the physiocrats, value is plagued by a degree of internal undecidability. For instance we find that Petty and Cantillon see land and labour as the sources from which wealth springs, while Turgot sees wealth springing only from labour. A similar contest arises when a third claimant on economic value emerges in the guise of the capitalist. For Ricardo land, labour and capital all add value, whereas Marx claims that value is produced by labour, which should be justly rewarded. Finally we see a similar split emerging as claims around the value of the entrepreneur are made. Schumpeter conjures an entrepreneur that is like a second face of the capitalist. This allows the 'undertaker' to make a claim on top of the payment of interest, rent, and wages. In contrast, Marshall and Knight attempt to attribute the entrepreneurial function to the bureaucratic executives who produce value through the management of uncertainty. These executives are then provided with a special wage for their labour as well as entrepreneurial profit for their management of uncertainty.

From these persistent splits in the attribution of value we are made aware of the fact that the value associated with particular economic actors is not something that is simply given. Rather, value is divided between a number of economic actors, and must be shared out amongst them. This means that the discursive constitution of which economic actors should be assigned a particular value, the clear and political and economic consequences of this are (at least potentially) open to dispute. But undervalued economic actors – such as labour at the present moment – are not doomed simply to be the victim of how the distribution of value is drawn up by elite economists like Schumpeter and enforced by his contemporary champions. Rather, it is possible to use the cracks that already exist in these value claims in order to further alternative claims on value. A clear and pragmatic example here might be workers making a claim that it is them, not the capitalist or manager, who has combined the factors of production in a novel fashion and therefore deserve to be rewarded for it with entrepreneurial profit. This active politics of advancing value claims demonstrates that economic discourse does not simply represent a set of value-creating activities but is actively implicated in making value claims in the context of an overall contest about the valuation of various activities.

Excavating the history of the valuation of the entrepreneur, we are drawing attention away from the obviousness of accumulation towards a more profound accumulation that we could call, with a nod towards Smith, 'previous accumulation' or 'primitive accumulation'. This is to say that, in the economic field, before Ricardo can set the goal of political economy as the discovery of the proper laws of distribution between land, labour and capital, there is a previous or primary valuation that identifies these three as sources of value. Equally, before we can ask how much value is added by the entrepreneur, we must accept the assumption that the entrepreneur is a source of value. An anti-essentialist reading of value will therefore not simply contest the amount of value allocated to various sources, but will trace the origins of each source and call into question the very status of claims that specific categories produce value.

Such an anti-essentialism of value should not be mistaken for a relativisation of value. Perhaps better would be to say that the ground-zero of value is analogous to what Freud calls a state of 'polymorphous perversity' (Freud, 1938: 592–3, see also Spivak, 1996: 121). This arises from the psychoanalytic suggestion that 'the constitutional sexual disposition of children is incomparably more variegated than might have been expected, that it deserves to be described as polymorphously perverse and that what is spoken of as the normal behaviour of the sexual function emerges from this disposition after certain of its components have been repressed' (Freud, 1979: 78). This is useful in that it indicates how the sources of value are far more variegated than allowed by most economic discourse, and that it is only through the injunction of a super-ego that this heterogeneous field is channelled and co-ordinated into a tidy and ordered space. There is much that could be done to extend these analogies via the analyses of Deleuze and Guattari (1983), who cast the social as polymorphously perverse, and suggest that it is only through the active intervention of 'desiring-production' that the social body takes on a semblance of unity. This unity can be a singular one, or it can consist of a tidily ordered rectangle of land, labour, capital and entrepreneurship.

WHO IS VALUABLE?

It is possible that some readers will be wondering what relevance any of this has to entrepreneurs in the 'real world'. Often it appears that economic discourse bears little relation to reality, and the writings of many academics only strengthen this impression. But while we have gone into some detail in debates on the vagaries of valuation in economic discourse, we want to suggest that this has the most immediate and practical relevance in economic life. This is because the kinds of valuations that are placed on various actors have the most material consequences, most obviously, of course, through the distribution of the wealth that is produced by economic activity. Clearly, valuation is a relational matter, in the sense that one thing is valuable only in relation to another thing that is less valuable. When it comes to the value that is put on the labourer, the landowner, the capitalist and the entrepreneur, these are not simply abstract economic categories. Concrete human subjects take up these subject positions, and in the process are themselves valued in relation to their ability to occupy these positions.

The practical consequence of these relational valuations of economic actors is laid bare if we compare the differential economic situation of entrepreneurs with those not lucky enough to be classed as such. Consider for example, a number of popular journalistic accounts of the realities of life for low-wage workers in advanced industrial economies (Abrams, 2002; Ehrenreich, 2002; Toynbee, 2003). All of these make very clear the fact that it is not a matter of not contributing sweat and blood, of working damn hard, that is the reason that this significant group is paid so little. It is to do with the cultural *valuations* that are placed on certain types of activity, or better, on certain groups of people. Because this is what remains intuitively plausible in the labour theory of value – that to the extent that each human being is valuable, their human activity when at work deserves to be valued. Of course, in contemporary capitalist societies, this is not the case. Some, who are able to combine the other factors of production in innovative ways, which is another way of saying that they are *in control of the production process*, are considered to be worthy of great rewards. And others, who have nothing but their labour to contribute are given, by comparison, very little indeed. Hence Ehrenreich's argument that:

> The 'working poor', as they are approvingly termed, are in fact the major philanthropists of our society. They neglect their own children so that the children of others will be cared for; they live in substandard housing so that other homes will be shiny and perfect; they endure privation so that inflation will be low and stock prices high. To be a member of the working poor is to be an anonymous donor, a nameless benefactor, to everyone else. (2002: 221)

The irony of the situation is that it is not 'everyone else' that is the beneficiary of the devaluation of certain types of activity. Because valuation is relational, it is those at the other end of the scale that have the most to gain from these relative valuations. If entrepreneurs gain from their relative valorisation in contemporary economies, those on the other side of the equation lose.

While the historical sketch that we have provided here remains little more than an outline of a genealogy of the value that is attributed to 'entrepreneurship' in economic discourse, we hope that at least one result of this analysis is clear. Looking critically at the history of the value that economic discourse has attributed to various actors we can see that there is no absolute grounding of claims to value. Valuation of economic actors is contingent, and is politically contested. This contestation takes place across a wide cultural space, and in this chapter we have perhaps underplayed alternative or resistant valuations of entrepreneurs. No matter how dominant it is, we could have spent less time discussing the way that economic discourse attributes value to this category of the entrepreneur, and spent more time looking at the way that this discourse is contested by those who find valuation of entrepreneurs to be one of the worst jokes that economists have ever told. To look at these contestations would involve another whole project, which will have to be done elsewhere. But what we have perhaps shown here is that entrepreneurs are not valued because they 'really' contribute value to economic activity. Rather, the entrepreneur is one of the fantasies of economic discourse, a fantasy which we might have begun to unmask.

5. Entrepreneurial excess

Questions of the differential value of entrepreneurship lead us to issues of inclusion and exclusion: Who gets to be an entrepreneur and who doesn't. We will deal with these questions directly in Chapters 6 and 7. But first of all, in this chapter we will look at the flipside of claims about the production of value we have just covered. In this chapter we will discuss issues of excess, consumption and wastage. As we will argue, these are an important part of a non-restrictive or 'general' conception of entrepreneurship. So as we turn to questions of irrational exuberance we will unmask the excessively rationalistic assumptions about entrepreneurship that are often made by functionalist, interpretive and critical researchers. Critical researchers have often objected to the extension of entrepreneurship into all public institutions and the concomitant rationalisation and depoliticisation of public life (du Gay, 2000b). As economic calculations come to override all others, there is a danger of public debate becoming dominated by calculation of input/output ratios, and thus discussion of substantive ends becomes almost totally excluded. According to critics of enterprise culture, economic life has become increasingly subject to a logic of 'performativity'. Diverse social actors including bureaucrats, academics, librarians, scientists, broadcasters and politicians increasingly take up the role of 'entrepreneur'. In doing so, they become actors who assess the world through a series of economic judgements. This logic appears so insidious that it spreads from its home in the small enterprise, through the modern corporation, into public and non-profit institutions and finally infests our own (previously) private lives.

One example of the extreme entrepreneurial mathematisation of everyday life was presented a few years ago by Jeffrey Pfeffer (2003), who with some embarrassment noted that a number of his colleagues at Stanford Business School assess the 'success' of their romantic interludes by calculating the amount spent during a date against the amount of 'payoff' they received from this investment. Of ultimate concern for critics of entrepreneurship is how such cold quantification could have taken over the landscape of our everyday life. Consequently, one of the tasks of a critique of entrepreneurship is constructed as that of expunging the logic of calculation from what we previously knew as private life.

While such a critique is potentially powerful, we are not sure whether it hits its target when it comes to a figure such as the entrepreneur. If we reflect on representations in economic thought and in the business press, we find that the entrepreneur hardly lives up to the critics' expectations. Instead of being careful calculators of profit and losses, entrepreneurs generally appear as deviant characters. They are usually not people who methodically assess input-output ratios, rather they are maverick, over-the-top, exuberant figures. This may mean that some critiques of enterprise culture have been misplaced, and that it is a mistake to charge the entrepreneur with the spread of an accountant's mentality. Rather than charging the entrepreneur with what Habermas (1984, 1987) calls the 'rationalization of the lifeworld', perhaps the unmasking of the entrepreneur might instead connect this hero of our age with exuberance, irrationality and excess.

We begin the chapter by identifying the place of excess in entrepreneurship discourse. We draw on a line of thought about excess and wastage that runs from Veblen's (1899) *Theory of the Leisure Class* and Mauss's (1950) *The Gift* towards Derrida's (1992b) *Given Time* and Bataille's (1989, 1991) *Accursed Share*. In these authors we find powerful explanations of how economies are not only characterised by a calculative logic of production, but also by incalculable consumption and excessive wastage. We go on to suggest that entrepreneurs, who over time have been attributed a positive valuation as shown in the previous chapter, have also been assigned the task of wasting a considerable portion of the excess produced by our society. We conclude with a discussion of the way that the small fragment of the population claiming to be 'entrepreneurs' makes a special claim on the right to waste, leaving to others the base activity of mere production.

THE PLACE OF EXCESS IN ENTREPRENEURSHIP

Casting an eye over the business press, we are confronted with endless waves of financial data and market reports. Sometimes this limitless sea is punctuated by a gigantic creature who leaps up from the deep. Some know this creature as the entrepreneur. Hence the journalists labouring at the *Financial Times* and the *Economist* do not recount stories of entrepreneurs as rational, calculating machines trawling the seas of financial capital. Instead, their shanties about entrepreneurs tell of unruly and elusive creatures who do not obey the rules of logical economic behaviour. These creatures embark on schemes for which they could not objectively predict the outcome. In undertaking such risky adventures they exercise not only their rational faculties, but act on gut feelings, hunches and mystical visions. This suggests, as we have argued in Chapter 3, that an understanding of the entrepreneur must include an account of how the entrepreneur is not an obvious thing but is rather a mysterious or sublime object.

Interestingly, recognition of the irrationality and exuberance of the entrepreneur can also be found in the mainstays of economic theory. One particularly important example appears in Joseph Schumpeter's *Theory of Economic Development*. In this book, Schumpeter develops a critique of the prevailing brand of economic thought at the time – marginal economics – which claimed that markets tend towards an equilibrium where profit, wages and rent naturally fall into balance with one another. Because marginalism sees the economy as something that tends towards stability, however, it is unable to explain one of the most fundamental characteristics of the capitalist economy – growth. Therefore, Schumpeter argued that a rationally balanced economy, where everyone shared the same information, paid the same profit, rent and wages and possessed the same technology, would be disastrous. If every offering on the market was essentially the same (because technology and other sources of competitive advantage were communally held), the only way that a firm could differentiate its products would be through cutting prices. Because all of the costs of production would be the same then the only cost that could be cut by the capitalist would be profit margins. Ultimately this would result in a declining rate of profit.

Schumpeter argued instead that the central dynamic of capitalism is accumulation and that a declining rate of profit could not go on forever. This led him to suggest, as we discussed in the previous chapter, that the capitalist economy continues to grow, not through a relatively well defined balance of land, labour and capital, but through the wilful destruction of the rational order previously established between the economic factors of production. This 'creative destruction' comes onto the scene in the form of the entrepreneur, who combines the factors of production in novel ways. By venturing new combinations the entrepreneur upsets the arrangements of production and thereby creates a disequilibrium in the economic system. Hence, for Schumpeter, the economy grows not at equilibrium but at disequilibrium, and it is the speculative entrepreneur who introduces this disequilibrium. The importance of the destructive activities of this entrepreneur is further sharpened in the dividing line Schumpeter draws between the entrepreneur and the manager. Here the entrepreneur is the character who brings together new combinations of the factors of production while the manager is the character who rationally administers existing factors of production, and ensures that they create the most efficient output. The entrepreneur, then, is the irrational destroyer of existing combinations of economic orders, whereas the manager is the rational administrator who attempts to draw out any value that can be extracted from the production arrangements already in place.

If we turn our gaze back to accounts of the entrepreneur in the business press, we also find stories of the fanciful speculations and personality quirks of famous entrepreneurs. We might find a description of how a loveable entrepreneur livens up their company by bouncing around the hallways on a spacehopper, wearing a Richard Nixon mask and yelling words of encouragement. Indeed, such excessive behaviour is so much a part of entrepreneurship discourse that we rarely bat an eyelid when it is described. In one biography of Richard Branson, for example, we find the following description:

> The company [Virgin] would take over some holiday hotel for three or four days of high jinks. This usually entailed Branson being the first to let off fire-extinguishers, initiate a food fight, or dress up in fish-net stockings and make-up for the inevitable fancy-dress party. (Brown, 1998: 198)

Thus, we see the extremism which is often taken to the point of absurdly unbelievable figures like Branson, and those who model themselves on him. In his autobiographical call to arms, *Screw It, Let's Do It*, Branson paints himself as not only a good person, but as the most extreme embodiment of good:

> When my sister Lindi and I were trying to sell copies of *Student* in the street, a tramp asked me for money. I didn't have a penny, but I was so fired up to do good, I tore off my clothes and gave them to him. I had to borrow a blanket before I was arrested. (2007: 176)

Excessive behaviour associated with the character of the entrepreneur can also be seen in various forms of outdoor adventuring. We are, again, quite used to hearing about the entrepreneur who is climbing Mount Everest or who has decided to venture to the North Pole or ride a camel train across the Sahara desert; all reminders that wealthy business owners enjoy pursuits that require the most costly equipment and achieve the greatest distance from the common masses. This entrepreneurial elite seems to prefer forms of disproportionate adventure that literally take them out of this world. Their exploits appear to express a barely contained desire to leave the profane world of lack and poverty through the most expensive means possible. Hence the popularity of heli-skiing, sky-diving, hang-gliding and similar activities.

In considering such adventuring, we might recall that the entrepreneur and the adventurer have in the past been fused characters. Indeed in Say's (1803) *Treatise on Political Economy*, we find that the entrepreneur is one who 'adventures' their capital and other possessions with the risk of no return. To illustrate his argument, Say makes liberal reference to the trader who sets off across the seas on a vessel and faces the very real chance of never returning. It is this genuine risk to life, limb and livelihood that makes the entrepreneur an adventurer. Many of today's entrepreneurs would, it appears, also like to consider themselves adventurers. Perhaps this is because the relentlessly systematic nature of much of their actual day-to-day activity does not require any such risk. To add an air of daring to their otherwise tawdry lives, entrepreneurs often seem intent on flinging themselves out on epic missions of destruction. One of the more glorious examples was the race between the late American entrepreneur Steve Fossett and the English entrepreneur Richard Branson to become the first person to fly around the world in a hot air balloon. In order to achieve this goal, vast sums of money were expended to pay for the necessary equipment and support. Fossett and Branson were, it seems, engaged in an authentic adventure and indeed failed a number of times, utterly squandering massive investments in their undertaking. They eventually teamed up, like old college buddies. Meanwhile, every time each or both of these adventurers landed in the sea, yet more resources were used up on rescue teams and replacement equipment.

What is fascinating about these forms of costly and wasteful adventure is that they aim at what seem to be utterly vacuous and empty purposes. They do not intend to increase the capacity of the entrepreneur's business, but are targeted at creating large-scale destruction of potentially productive resources for absolutely no end. What is even more interesting is that this excessive expenditure is apparently not considered to be some kind of extra-curricular activity that these entrepreneurs participate in during their days off. No, narratives surrounding the aforementioned race to be the first entrepreneur who has spent scores of millions of dollars attempting to fly around the world in a hot air balloon discussed this endeavour as if it were something internal to the entrepreneurial characteristics of risk taking, desiring-achievement and having vision. Apparently it is not because Fossett or Branson were curious human beings or had a particular interest in aviation that they were motivated to embark on such an expedition. Instead it is because they were *entrepreneurs* that they launched this outlandish adventure.

But one of the problems that we immediately face when trying to understand such entrepreneurial excess is the way that even the most apparently excessive actions are often described as something other than excessive. In this respect we could consider the case of Dennis Tito, the Californian financial entrepreneur who, in April 2001, became the first person to pay to travel into space. Sixty-year-old Tito took an eight-day trip on the Russian Soyuz spacecraft, spending six days on the International Space Station, in orbit around the earth. This cost him US$20 million. What is interesting about his case is not simply the excessive expenditure itself, but the justification that was given to the expenditure. Tito insisted that the space expedition was not just a vacation, and he was not doing it out of his own self-seeking motives. Rather, at times he reduced it to little more than a part of his continuing professional development. 'It's not going to be a holiday' he stressed in one interview, 'to me it is a life's dream and the start of a new career' (quoted in BBC News, 2001). But beyond his own personal development, Tito justified the trip in terms of the benefits that others would gain from him taking it. Almost philanthropically, he insisted that 'What I am doing is actually helping the cash-starved Russian space programme and actually helping the ISS [International Space Station]' (quoted in CBS News, 2001). However, in case we thought that a cash gift to the Russian space programme and the International Space Station was all that Tito was giving, he was also (by his own account at least) working towards democratising space travel by being an adventurer in the name of the masses. As he put it,

> If you look back at the early days of powered flight, the wealthy people were the ones who could afford to go in an airplane 80, 90 years ago. It was that interest that ultimately led to the development of commercial aviation, where everyone could afford it. Now it might be another 50 or 80 years before it gets down to a reasonable price. But that's how it starts. (Tito, quoted in CBS News, 2001)

One might wonder if it is not a little ridiculous to assess any and all excessive expenditure as ultimately productive. Should we not be more honest and approach these spending sprees as what they plainly seem to be – acts of excess? Instead of seeing the abyss of destruction that lies at the heart of the entrepreneur as ultimately productive, perhaps we need to think again. Perhaps we need to take this core of destruction, waste and excess as another opportunity for unmasking the entrepreneur. Therefore, to move towards an explanation of entrepreneurial excess, in the next two sections we will look at some ways of theorising excess. First we will look at its social functions, as outlined by Veblen and Mauss, and then turn to a critique of such ideas, using Derrida and Bataille.

THE SOCIAL FUNCTIONS OF EXCESS

Thorstein Veblen's *Theory of the Leisure Class* begins with a speculative historical anthropology of the emergence of what he calls 'the leisure class'. In the opening chapters Veblen sketches a set of historical changes in the structure of work in 'barbarian' and 'primitive' societies. In these societies a basic distinction emerges between different types of work, a distinction that continues today in class societies. This continuity is important for Veblen, as 'The institution of a leisure class is the outgrowth of an early discrimination between employments, according to which some employments are worthy and others are unworthy' (1899: 25). A differentiation thereby arises between what Veblen calls 'exploit' and 'drudgery'. Exploit includes any sort of glamorous and high-status activity, usually reserved exclusively for men, activities such as 'warfare, politics, public worship, and public merrymaking' (Veblen, 1899: 26). By contrast, drudgery refers to the mundane activity of labour, the routine and low-status activity of producing the material bases of life.

In addition to his emphasis on the historical continuity of this distinction, Veblen offers an understanding of the means through which it is symbolised and hence reproduced. He argues that in primitive societies those bearing the mark of 'exploit' initially display their capacity for this in their bodily activities, their natural strength and endurance, but later turn to other means to represent their virility to others. Hence the tradition of the use of weapons and armour to suggest strength, the honorific epithets deployed to describe great leaders, and the depiction of 'rapacious beasts and birds of prey' (Veblen, 1899: 31) in heraldry through to the present day. For Veblen, the important function of these displays is a symbolic one. That is to say, the finely crafted sword or the imagery of a lion on a flag serve as an attempt to symbolise the capacity for exploit of their bearer.

While this kind of historical sketch is obviously open to all manner of objections, it is not its verisimilitude but what it shows us about the present that renders it productive. What is significant is how Veblen demonstrates the historical continuity of the division between drudgery and exploit in the light of changing symbolic representations of this distinction. In contrast to slave and feudal economies, Veblen notes that in modern capitalist economies

> the opportunities for gaining distinction by means of this direct manifestation of superior force grow less available both in scope and frequency. At the same time the opportunities for industrial aggression, and for the accumulation of property by the quasi-peaceable methods of nomadic industry, increase in scope and availability. (1899: 37)

With this shift, the possession of economic wealth increasingly comes to operate as an abstract signifier, standing in for the ability of its holder to 'exploit'. Hence the modern businessperson need not have any physical capacity, and certainly need not bear arms, to ensure that their strength is recognised. Instead, 'When accumulated goods have in this way become the accepted badge of efficiency, the possession of wealth presently assumes the character of an independent and definitive basis of esteem' (Veblen, 1899: 37). In this context, Veblen describes the practices of the modern leisure class, most famously represented in the practice of what he calls 'conspicuous consumption'. This is a form of excessive consumption that satisfies no obviously recognisable need but rather enhances the status of the subject who engages in it. Veblen's analysis therefore presents the possibility of thinking about the place of excessive consumption in reproducing relations of production, even if he does not take this theme as far as he might. He also makes an important contribution by drawing attention to the social function of something that appears to be excessive – in our case the conspicuous consumption of the entrepreneur. We can take his considerations further by turning to the work of Mauss, Derrida and Bataille.

Marcel Mauss's famous discussion of the social functions of excessive expenditure appear in his well-known essay *The Gift* (1950). Here he explores the place of giving in 'primitive' and modern societies. Mauss notes that we tend to think of giving as something diametrically opposed to relations of trade or exchange. Common sense tells us that when we *trade* or *exchange* an item we expect to gain something in return. But when we *give* it, we expect nothing back. Mauss challenges this view by arguing that, when we give, we often set up an obligation for the receiver to return a favour at some later time. What this means is that there is no such thing as a free gift. Instead, giving is always bound up with relations of implied reciprocation.

One particularly intriguing type of gift given by some societies is embodied in the potlatch, which is taken from a word used by Northwest American Indians meaning 'to feed' or 'to consume' (Mauss, 1950: 7). In potlatch festivals a tribe takes fine goods that have been painstakingly constructed and lavishly destroys them in front of members of a neighbouring tribe. What is interesting is that the neighbouring tribe who witnesses the potlatch will later reciprocate. Indeed the central obligation of the potlatch is that one gives, one receives and then reciprocates (Mauss, 1950: 50–55). The implication is that while we might immediately assume that the potlatch is purely excessive expenditure, a giving without expecting anything in return, we are quite wrong. Instead, when one commits the precious materials of one's village to a local river, one expects a reciprocal gift of destruction from the neighbouring village. What we therefore have is a kind of exchange of excessive destruction, or what Mauss calls a 'gift economy'. Moreover, this gift economy is not simply an unnecessary feature of the society in question. For Mauss it serves an ultimately useful function. The effect of these exchanges of destruction is the building of social solidarity, suggesting that acts of wastage are not socially deviant but instead centrally important to building cohesion.

Veblen and Mauss both clearly contribute to the way that we might understand entrepreneurial excess. Following Veblen, conspicuously excessive behaviour serves a primitive function as a marker of distinction, indicating how far the exploits of the entrepreneur are above 'drudgery', and the way that they give the entrepreneur an air of mystery and transcendence. Following Mauss, even the most apparently ludicrous acts of wastage serve a latent function, which is one of cohesion or solidarity in which the viewing of a spectacle can bring people together. Nonetheless, and while both of these explanations have considerable force, we propose to look a little further than we are taken by understandings based on the idea of the social functions of excess. To do this we will turn to some thinkers who have seen excess, not as part of a circle of such functions, but as something that breaks that circle.

THE BROKEN CIRCLE

We find a movement away from the social functions of excess in works like Jacques Derrida's *Given Time* (1992b). In this book Derrida questions the notion that giving functions in a circular way, and shows how the gift actually threatens to fracture the circle of exchange. The gift is something that operates in relation to economy, to be sure. But Derrida stresses the way that the gift *breaks* the circle of economy. If there is anything that is to be truly *given*, then the giver must not expect anything in return. Otherwise, strictly speaking, the gift is not a gift, but is merely part of a ritual system of exchange. If anything, a gift that is given with the expectation of return gives nothing but time. That is, it gives the receiver time to prepare a gift which can be returned in recompense. But a gift is a thing that strictly speaking breaks both the circle of economy and the circle of time. It breaks out from the system of exchange, and hence always implies a certain madness, defying reason and exceeding expectations of return. In this way, the gift

> must not circulate, it must not be exchanged, it must not in any case be exhausted, as a gift, by the process of exchange, by the movement of circulation of the circle in the form of return to the point of departure. If the figure of the circle is essential to economics, the gift must remain *aneconomic*. (Derrida, 1992b: 7)

Derrida exposes the limits of the thinking about the gift and excess that we find in Mauss. He is concerned in particular with the way that Mauss converts the gift and the potlatch into socially functional acts. When he discusses the ritual practices of giving and wastage among 'primitive' peoples,

Mauss is rightly concerned to avoid the ethnocentric assumption that such practices are simply irrational, which would be to impose a Western conception. Hence he seeks out the functions, the purpose, the reason and the logic of the gift and the potlatch. In doing so he locates their ostensible social effects, and so places the potlatch within the figure of a circle. Nevertheless, Derrida exposes the irony of Mauss's work on the gift. He even goes so far as to say that a work as monumental as *The Gift* speaks of everything but the gift: 'It deals with economy, exchange, contract (*do et des*), it speaks of raising the stakes, sacrifice, gift *and* countergift – in short, everything that in the thing itself impels the gift *and* the annulment of the gift' (Derrida, 1992b: 24).

In this way Derrida locates behind Mauss's apparent anti-ethnocentrism a deeper and more profound prejudice. Although Mauss wants to avoid the assumption that the potlatch is irrational (which is how it may appear, at first glance, to Western eyes), he ends up attributing a rationality and functionality to these practices of waste. In doing so, Mauss returns the potlatch to economy, and hence encloses it within the figure of the circle. He thereby introduces an ethnocentrism that belies his seeming relativism. Indeed, in his efforts to avoid a culturally bound construction that would see the practices of others as inherently irrational, Mauss actually makes a *profoundly* Western and capitalistic assumption – that all practices, particularly economic ones, have a reason, a rationality and an expectation of return. Against this, Derrida positions the gift as 'the very figure of the impossible' (1992b: 7), and recalls that not all things have a purpose, a function or a rationale.

We find another important way of thinking outside of the circle in the work of Georges Bataille (1985, 1989, 1991). One of Bataille's objections to twentieth-century social thought was that it assumed a form of 'productivism'. That is, social thought has been obsessed with the category of production, and tends to explain all human activity in terms of what it contributes to the expansion of available resources. We are adept at seeing anything from childbirth to capital punishment as an exercise in production. Economists may therefore regard the hot-air-ballooning entrepreneur as producing wages for rescue workers, balloon makers and developers of global positioning systems, and even generating the advertising revenue associated with worldwide news audiences. For Bataille, however, this productivism is a fundamental mistake because it only takes into account a fraction of the economy. In order to develop a broader conceptualization of the economy he argues that we must move beyond a myopic focus on production and look at processes of consumption. Doing so does not mean that we merely need to attend to how our entrepreneur builds their sense of worth through purchasing particular commodities. This leaves us within the circle of the non-excessive, that is to say 'productive' consumption. If we accept Bataille's plea for a widened concept of consumption, we are faced with the question of its purposes – and in order to answer this question we need to comprehend his critique of economy.

To clarify what he means by 'economy', Bataille draws on Mauss's widened concept of the total service economy to argue for a contrast between the *restrictive* and the *general* economy. The former consists of what we would normally consider within economics – namely the interchange of goods and services, particularly when they have a price attached to them. In place of this restrictive conceptualisation of the economy Bataille argues that, to understand the processes of consumption and production, it is also necessary to see how the economy is bound up with its broader surroundings. This goes even further than Mauss's inquiry into the exchange of goods, services and honour. For Bataille, a general economy in fact extends beyond human exchange and includes 'the movement of energy on the earth' (1989: 10). This broader understanding allows Bataille to bring an all-encompassing range of phenomena – including the sun's rays, the growth of a calf, festivals, eroticism, warfare and sacrifice – into the economic equation as involving the flow or, perhaps more importantly, the consumption of energy.

It is through this conceptualisation of the general economy that Bataille outlines the 'basic fact' of consumption; that is, because any organism tends to produce more energy than it needs (otherwise it dies), the fundamental economic problem is in fact how this excess energy will be consumed:

> The living organism, in a situation determined by the play of energy on the surface of the globe, ordinarily receives more energy than is necessary for maintaining life; the excess energy (wealth) can be used for the growth of the system (e.g., an organism); if the system can no longer grow, or if the excess cannot be completely absorbed, it must necessarily be lost without profit; it must be spent, willingly or not, gloriously or catastrophically. (Bataille, 1989: 21)

In this passage we find the question that orients the three volumes of Bataille's *Accursed Share* – how organisms waste and how they expend the energy that they have accumulated. This involves demonstrating how destruction and excessive expenditure are central problems faced by all human societies. Indeed, he contends that the squandering of excess through luxury is so central that 'the history of life on earth is mainly the effect of a wild exuberance' (Bataille, 1989: 33), and goes on to argue that what defines a society is not its mode of production, but rather its surplus and how it disposes of that surplus (Bataille, 1989: 106).

ENTREPRENEURIAL EXCESS AND CLASS STRUGGLE

Such considerations of the gift and excess certainly turn many concepts of the economy on their head. No longer is economic activity seen in terms of its utility. Rather, we find a general economy beneath the productive economy, one of ceaseless consumption and excessive expenditure. Given the examples of entrepreneurial excess we have discussed above, it is clear that the figure of the entrepreneur is defined by a certain excessiveness and is an important marker of the continuation of the potlatch today. Although Bataille argues that American capitalism in particular is marked by productivism, the contemporary economy actually involves ways of configuring excessive expenditure, and the entrepreneur is central to this.

We should also recall that this process involves antagonism or, to put it simply, class struggle. As Bataille insisted, excess, even though it might have a social function, 'immediately leads to an agonistic and apparently antisocial act of separation' (1985: 125). In a way that is reminiscent of Veblen, then, Bataille emphasises the way that excess involves conflict. As he puts it, bourgeois society

> gives the workers rights equal to those of the masters, and it announces this *equality* by inscribing that word on walls. But the masters, who act as if they were the expression of society itself, are preoccupied – more seriously than with any other concern – with showing that they do not in any way share the abjection of the men they employ. *The end of the workers' activity is to produce in order to live, but the bosses' activity is to produce in order to condemn the working producers to a hideous degradation* – for there is no disjunction possible between, on the one hand, the characterization the bosses seek through their modes of expenditure, which tend to elevate themselves above human baseness, and on the other hand this baseness itself, of which this characterization is a function. (Bataille, 1985: 125–6)

It should be clear, then, that Bataille's emphasis on expenditure does not abandon an interest in relations of production, nor does it ignore the place of class struggle in capitalist societies. Rather, it positions expenditure within that struggle and contestation, and shows that expenditure is a crucial part of the political economy. So, while noting that excessive expenditure is a part of all societies, he gives us concepts for thinking about the way that excess is configured in different societies.

Critically, he draws attention to the way that differences of distribution involve a political economy of excess. Faced with this, and recognizing that excess is central to entrepreneurship, the question becomes one of thinking critically about the distribution of entrepreneurial excess. From the examples discussed above, we see that entrepreneurial excess is localised in a particular individual, the entrepreneur. Today it is the entrepreneur, amongst a few others, who is given the hallowed role of consuming and destroying the precious resources which the most advanced industrial societies produce. In the process of being entrepreneurial, it seems that they must engage in excessive activities like throwing parties, destroying industries and engaging in endless rounds of golf. Indeed, it seems to be precisely these behaviours that define the character of the entrepreneur. The almost erotic quality that is afforded to this figure is given a luxurious lustre by its excessiveness – it is precisely because the entrepreneur attracts such a massive amount of resources for the purpose of excessive expenditure that their character is all the more desirable.

Perhaps, then, the real job description of the entrepreneur is not so much management of production (which would in any case only generate a managerial wage): instead, it is the management of wilful destruction. In other words, the entrepreneur receives an 'entrepreneurial profit' for being a vortex of excess. As a corollary, one might suspect that, if Bataille had witnessed the contemporary culture of enterprise, he may have prepared an additional chapter for *Accursed Share*. This would document how the entrepreneur has become a central focus of excessive expenditure in contemporary capitalist society. Instead of pleasing the gods through excessive construction and production, today we apparently plunge massive resources into the impossible task of 'being entrepreneurial'. And in plunging these resources into such pursuits, our entrepreneurial culture favours the very small portion of the population who make it.

GENEROSITY

To further draw out the implications of the political economy of excess, there is much that we can take from the arguments made by Rosalyn Diprose in her book *Corporeal Generosity* (2002). Drawing on but also extending the arguments made by some of the thinkers that we have considered here, in particular Derrida, and also deploying recent critical thinking around the gift (see, for example, Schrift, 1997; Wyschogrod et al., 2002), Diprose elaborates a politicised conception of the giving of bodies. While Derrida's thinking about the gift opens up critically important questions about the possibilities of ethics and justice (Derrida, 1992b, see also 1992a, 1995; Jones, 2003), Diprose articulates Derrida's thinking of the gift in terms of *injustice*. The issue here becomes one of which gifts are recognised as such and, crucially, which are not seen as gifts. Often invisibility occurs because some gifts are thought to take place in a circle, an 'economy' in the sense we have discussed above. Diprose draws attention to gifts that are not recognised as gifts and shows how this, far from being an unusual or rare thing, permeates social and economic practice. The corporeal element of her argument is to show how certain types of body are treated as if it is natural for them to give, and hence their giving is rendered invisible. Other types of body are assumed to not normally give, and hence their normal or even excessive acts are rendered as 'gifts'. This involves a complex social process of the recognition and forgetting of various acts of generosity by different actors: 'the asymmetrical forgetting of generosity at the foundation of social injustice depends on the asymmetrical evaluation of different bodies. Some bodies accrue value, identity, and recognition through accumulating the gifts of others and at their expense' (Diprose, 2002: 9).

In the previous chapter we outlined a genealogy of the valuation of the entrepreneur, noting that one of the ways of claiming value is through claims to be an entrepreneur. Extending this argument, in this chapter we have looked at the way that entrepreneurs are able to mobilise claims to excessive expenditure, the most basic point being that the excesses of entrepreneurs are generally not conceived of as such. It is claimed instead (and whether these claims are successful or not is a difficult question) that they are not excessive at all. In many cases, such as Tito's space odyssey, it is claimed that they serve a social function. As should now be clear, we sense that these claims are rather suspect, and disguise a more profound, and more problematic, dynamic of the asymmetrical valuation of different bodies. This is important because the entrepreneur is a vortex that destroys the excesses of our globally interconnected economy, while others live across the borders, starving, thirsty and sick. What egalitarian case can be made for the handful of entrepreneurs at a lavish dinner to impress a corporate client, squandering what is equivalent to the earnings of a lifetime for many others on the planet?

Perhaps a solution to entrepreneurial excess, such as committing all resources to productive endeavours, is impossible. There is always excess. Some resources are always wasted. If this is so, then the question becomes how we choose to collectively waste our resources, and how excessive expenditure is justified. As we have argued above, in societies such as ours, the entrepreneur is one of the central loci of excessive consumption. Anyone who is able to attach themselves to the notion of entrepreneur might be able to participate in this entrepreneurial potlatch. But not all bodies are successful in their attempts to be an 'adventuring entrepreneur'; and distribution of excess to the minority who are successful is not inevitable or necessary, but socially, historically and politically determined. If it is possible to change the distribution of excess, then this would involve not simply returning ourselves to a circle of production, but constructing a different political economy of excess.

6. Is the Marquis de Sade an entrepreneur?

Entrepreneurship is not an obvious, stable or present object. Rather, it is a place-holder in the history of political and economic struggle over valuation and the right to waste. If to successfully claim 'I am an entrepreneur' brings remarkable benefits, then we need now to give an account of the symbolic universe in which such claims to be entrepreneurial are coded as plausible or implausible. Thus in this chapter and the next we will examine two unlikely entrepreneurs – the Marquis de Sade and the illegal immigrant. By showing that the exclusion of these categories from entrepreneurship is implausible, we will further unmask the entrepreneur, and seek what else lurks barely beneath the designer suit. In this chapter we give this a twist by taking up what might appear at first to be an 'extreme' case of entrepreneurship. We ask if the infamous Marquis de Sade, from whom we take the reference to modern 'sadism', is an entrepreneur. Our analysis seeks to demonstrate that, if we analyse Sade in terms of social or institutional entrepreneurship, this case is not so far fetched as it might first seem. In fact, we argue that Sade can only be *not* seen as an entrepreneur if we overestimate his failures and, moreover, if we assume a particular morality and fail to pay enough attention to economics.

It is important to stress that methodologically we are concerned here to bring to centre stage the question of *exclusion* in entrepreneurship. There is a lot of talk today about seeing entrepreneurship more broadly, about focusing on social entrepreneurship and institutional entrepreneurship. But our question here is somewhat different. For us, the crucial question concerning the politics of entrepreneurship is not simply 'who is an entrepreneur?', but 'who is *not* an entrepreneur?' Our concern therefore is to ask who gets excluded from entrepreneurship, and why.

We ask these questions in order to unmask the underlying morality and politics of entrepreneurship, and not so that we could expand entrepreneurship and thereby start describing anyone and anything in terms of entrepreneurship. One problem with entrepreneurship discourse is that it tries to take over everything, to make everything and everybody 'entrepreneurial'. Overgeneralisation of a very partial concept is of course a great danger. But the flipside is also a great risk, and this is why we here want to account for those who are excluded from entrepreneurship in the first place. This is why we take up the apparently implausible case of the Marquis de Sade. Our goal is not to make more space in entrepreneurship discourse for cases such as Sade. Rather, our intention here is essentially critical and involves unmasking the pretensions of entrepreneurship discourse. It is possible to learn from Sade not an expanded conception of entrepreneurship, but rather the precise limits of entrepreneurship discourse, its pretences and its politics. We advance Sade as not simply a strange case, but as an example that calls into question the inability of entrepreneurship discourse to account for failure, economics and ethics.

The association of Sade and entrepreneurship is far from random, as we hope you will soon see. It is a part of common language in the workplace, such as 'My boss is a sadist' or 'You don't have to be a masochist to work here, but it certainly helps!'. But beyond these common throwaways, there is now a small body of literature that takes more seriously the task of drawing on Sade, or more generally on sadomasochism, to understand management, organisation and work (Burrell, 1997; Brewis and Linstead, 2000; Cederström and Grassman, 2007; Stubbs, 2005; ten Bos, 2006). We take up Sade in order to take entrepreneurship to its limits, and in doing so to clarify that which it disavows but cannot repress.

ENTREPRENEURSHIP AT ITS LIMITS

There are certain moments in history when there is an explosion of entrepreneurial activity. This typically involves individuals and groups vigorously challenging existing rules, constructing new institutions, developing new norms and new ways of thinking. Some times and places when this has occurred include the Renaissance period in the Italian city-states, the Low Countries during the sixteenth century, Victorian England, nineteenth-century United States, early twentieth-century Russia and Eastern Europe after 1989. Each of these moments was characterised by a fundamental and discontinuous shock to existing systems. Such events provide an opportunity for entrepreneurs to construct new markets, establish new forms of organisation and articulate new ideas. Indeed, studies of entrepreneurship remind us that fundamental discontinuous changes in existing institutions is one of the surest sparks to ignite entrepreneurship (Tarrow, 1998; Campbell, 2004).

Perhaps one of the most compressed and tumultuous explosions of various forms of entrepreneurship was during the French revolution of 1789 (for a standard account see Lefebvre, 1967). The revolution not only swept away the *ancien régime*, but also provided widespread opportunities for 'institutional entrepreneurship' (see Hardy and Maguire, 2008). Some of these projects of institutional entrepreneurship included the establishment of classical French cuisine (Ferguson, 1998), the rise of the modern social movements (Tilly, 1986), the creation of a rationally planned inner city with large avenues (Benjamin, 2002), the development of a modern sewerage system (Laporte, 2000), the creation of the modern medical clinic, prison and asylum (Foucault, 1973, 1977, 2005), and the creation of the *Grande Ecole* system of higher education (Osbourne, 1983), to name just a few. These diverse and widespread achievements certainly reveal the spirit of liberty and the dynamics of 'creative destruction' that are unleashed by large-scale social upheavals. Each of these enterprises also appears to be undergirded by a common commitment to liberation from tradition through the institution of rational schemes.

As we know, the entrepreneurial spirit knows no bounds. The demands for reform in one sector of life lead to demands for the reconstruction of another sector of social life. Hence a kind of serial and widespread institutional entrepreneurship. As well as offering the possibility of fundamentally transforming the institutions of government, education, and exchange, the revolution also offered an opportunity to reconstruct the institutions of, for example, sexuality. There were a range of reform projects that made sex into a public issue that was subject to a whole range of techniques, professions and bodies of professional knowledge, as has been famously described by Foucault (1978). This reform process was prefigured by the introduction of the Christian pastoral confessional practices promoted by budding institutional entrepreneurs within the Catholic Church in France. These new confessional practices encouraged worshippers to 'confess everything' and make sexual behaviour into an object of discourse and reflection. This was built on immediately before and after the revolution through three projects (Foucault, 1978). First, this involved demographers making sex into an object of surveillance and policing through monitoring and intervening in rates of national birth and population. The second project involved the intervention of educators, who developed a whole series of technologies and bodies of rules around the monitoring of childhood sexuality. The final project that sought to reform institutions of sexuality involved the medical fraternity developing a whole specialist body of knowledge and intervention. The target of medical efforts became the sexuality of women, children, deviants, perverts and other 'abnormals' (Foucault, 2003). Overarching each of these efforts was 'a regulated and polymorphous incitement to discourse' (Foucault, 1978: 34) which attempted to create a rational science of sexuality. Thus what we observe is a similar attempt by a series of institutional entrepreneurs to liberate French society from the 'traditional sexuality' of medieval Europe and replace it with a rational, regulated sexuality.

This movement to reconstruct sexuality did not only involve those 'decent' citizens who sought carefully to ensure a respectable and controlled bourgeois sexuality. It also provided an ideal opportunity for a loose literary movement known as the libertines to put forward their own version of sexual reform. The libertines sought to take the revolution at its word and press for absolute liberty in the institution of sexuality and pleasure (Feher, 1997). What is interesting about the libertines for our purposes is the fact that they were an extreme example of institutional entrepreneurs. In this chapter we propose to investigate this strange example of taking innovation too far. Focusing on the most notorious libertine, the Marquis de Sade, we reveal striking resemblances between his visions of liberation and those valorised by contemporary entrepreneurship theory and practice. We argue that what is disturbing about Sade is that he takes the logic of entrepreneurship too far, showing up some of the horrific possibilities of entrepreneurship in the extreme.

SADE, LIBERTINE

In many ways, the libertine is the other side of the nineteenth-century medical practitioner. Instead of advocating the careful restriction of sex, the libertine passionately proposes the opposite and seeks a radical multiplication of sexual acts and debauchery. In place of the technologies of inspection proposed by the medical fraternity, the libertine agitates for the technology of the orgy. Like the medical, demographic and educational reformers, libertines produced a veritable explosion of discourse around sexuality. But instead of seeking to instil a 'normal' sexuality based around the conjugal family, they advocated revelry in sexual pleasure. Instead of complex rules around the sexual education of children, the classification of various types of sexual perversities, or the development of plans to increase birth rates, the libertine provides a different kind of description. This is a detailed description of sexual liaisons of all, and indeed *every*, kind.

To be sure, libertinage is certainly not a movement unique to revolutionary France. The word is derived from the Latin, *libertus,* which means 'freedman'. It entered into common parlance during the sixteenth century and was largely associated with atheism. However, by the eighteenth century, libertinage became associated with debauchery. The result was that by the end of the eighteenth century, libertinage denoted 'a way of thinking and living that evoked sexual freedom, seduction and frivolity' (Cusset, 1998: 2). The 'successful' sexual reforms typically focused on the transformation of sexuality through social institutions such as the school, the hospital and systems of public administration. By contrast, libertinage was largely a literary and artistic movement which sought to challenge and perhaps reform the cultural institutions associated with sexuality. As students of neo-institutional theory would claim, this is largely achieved through shifts in the discourses which are used to talk and think about a phenomenon (Phillips et al., 2004). The libertines sought to achieve such shifts in discourse through circulating a range of scandalous litera-ture. Well-known representatives of libertine literature include Marivaux, Crébillon, Laclos, and Sade.

We should note that the libertine movement is typically thought of as a bridge between the excesses of the *ancien régime* and the bloody fervour of the revolution. Indeed, aristocratic excess is a favoured subject matter in much libertine literature. We should also note that the libertine movement was by no means a well-connected network of authors working towards a common goal. It was instead a series of individual authors, working across more than a century, whose work showed at least a common concern with celebrating debauchery. This means that there are important differences between what different libertines advocated. Perhaps the most striking one is between writers such as Crébillon, who advocated losing oneself to the moment of surprise and physical pleasure, and writers like Laclos and Sade, who emphasised the need for self-control and purposeful and rational pursuit and organisation of pleasure (Cusset, 1998: 2). What we therefore seem to have is a movement with two opposing models to guide the reform and radicalisation of sexuality. On the one hand, there are those who advocate a reform of sexuality through generalised abandonment to sexual whims. On the other hand, there are those who advocate a rational and highly organised pursuit of sexual satisfaction. It is this second model which perhaps gained the most ground following the revolution, and it is to this model we shall turn our attention.

Perhaps the pre-eminent example of the extreme rational pursuit of sexual pleasure can be found in the work of Donatien Alphonse François de Sade (1740–1814), better known as the Marquis de Sade. Sade was a French aristocrat who first came to public attention for his sexual miscon-duct with young prostitutes and household employees of both sexes. This led to a series of imprisonments and confinements in asylums through-out his life. Sade also played an active role in the revolution. According to Sadian legend, a few days prior to the storming of the Bastille, Sade goaded crowds from his window in the Bastille by claiming that prison-ers were being murdered inside. He later took up a number of official positions within the revolutionary government and a seat in the National Convention. During Sade's long stays in prison he produced a range of plays and novels, the best known of which are *Dialogue Between a Priest and a Dying Man* (1782), *120 Days of Sodom* (1785), *Justine* (1791), *Philosophy in the Bedroom* (1795), and *Juliette* (1798). While Sade's literary outpourings were influential during post-revolutionary France, they quickly fell into ill repute, only to be recovered during the middle of the twentieth century through promotion by a range of literary champions such as Maurice Heine and Gilbert Lely and prominent intellectuals of the time such as Simone de Beauvoir (1966), Georges Bataille (2001), Jacques Lacan (2006b), Pierre Klossowski (1966) and Maurice Blanchot (1967). In 1975, Sade was again the topic of public disgust following the release of Pier Paolo Pasolini's film version of *Salo, or, The 120 Days of Sodom*. Today, Sade is considered to be one of the central exemplars of the libertine movement in French literature.

Because the efforts and impact of Sade were largely literary in nature, we will emphasise his literary works at the expense of a fuller treatment of his engagements with the political institutions of the republic. In Sade's literary works we find striking parallels with other attempts to reconstruct institutions in France following the revolution. Central to these efforts are claims to liberty and rationality which, we argue, continue to be at the heart of contemporary entrepreneurship discourse. However, what is interesting about Sade is that he takes these discourses to their extreme. By taking the discourse of liberty to its limits, Sade alerts us to the pathologies and possibilities that lie at the heart of calls to free enterprise.

Before proceeding, we should be clear that we are making no effort here to celebrate or glorify Sade or his writing. Instead we are using Sade as an example of someone who takes the promises of enterprise to its limits. Indeed we propose to present Sade as an 'abject' figure. By this we mean an object that is simultaneously attractive and disgusting, which catches one in 'a vortex of summons and repulsion', which Kristeva explains is like an 'inescapable boomerang' that might be thrown away only to return (Kristeva, 1984: 1). It is this kind of object that we earlier described as 'the sublime object of entrepreneurship', and here is figured in all of its abjectness. By engaging with a figure who pushes the logic of entrepreneurship too far, we are able to tease out the morality and politics lurking beneath the mask of entrepreneurship.

SADE, ENTREPRENEUR

On the face of it, the idea that an aristocratic libertine who spent over half his life in prison is an entrepreneur is patently ridiculous. If we applied Schumpeter's definition of the entrepreneur as the character who creates novel combinations of the factors of production and is rewarded with an entrepreneurial profit (Schumpeter, 1934), then Sade and his fellow libertines would certainly be instantly dismissed from consideration. Indeed, in many respects Sade is quite the opposite of the entrepreneur that Schumpeter describes. He was a member of the aristocracy, which meant he was not compelled to engage in any serious ventures of his own capital, nor did he engage in labour, nor attempt to devise a novel combination of land, labour and capital. Rather he lived exclusively off rents from lands that he inherited from his father. Nor could we say that Sade was a great champion of economic entrepreneurship as such. Indeed, following the revolution he authored and circulated a revolutionary pamphlet entitled *Frenchmen! One More Effort If You Wish to Be Republicans*, in which he advocated the abolition of private property. Such bold claims to institutional innovation are not typically associated with the successful entrepreneur.

But despite these two notable cleavages between Sade and the entrepreneur, we can recognise in him some of the aspects widely associated with entrepreneurs and entrepreneurship. In particular, note his distaste for established institutions, his seizure of opportunity, his inclination to radical thinking and radical solutions, his willingness to ruthlessly organise, and above all his attempts to change dominant patterns of organisation. So perhaps instead of suggesting that Sade is an economic entrepreneur, we might see him as a kind of institutional entrepreneur.

According to the growing literature on the topic, an institutional entrepreneur is an individual or group who seeks to establish new institutions or transform existing institutions (Eisenstadt, 1964; Hardy and Maguire, 2008). In many ways Sade's efforts can be seen as an attempt to intervene violently in the existing institutions of his day surrounding sexuality and to reconstruct them. To be sure, Sade neither attempted to transform existing rules around sexuality, nor did he mobilize significant resources in this effort, nor attempt to build any plausible institutions such as a libertine community. What he did do, however, was seek to challenge the dominant patterns of thinking about the sexuality of his time through his shocking and scandalous work. This involved an attempt to transform what institutionalists call 'the cognitive schemas' (Scott, 1999) which instituted a particular form of sexuality. However, unlike most skilled institutional entrepreneurs (for example, Fligstein, 1997; Garud et al., 2002), Sade was patently unskilled in coalition building. In fact his tactics led to the instant dissolution of any coalition which might form around him. He was unlikeable, and unliked. But this has not stopped entrepreneurs in the past, and Sade also took a different path than likeability. The thing that made Sade into a serious 'institutional entrepreneur' was his ability to propagate scandalous and shocking discourses in the field of debates about sexuality. Just as, following the revolution, elite chefs sought to change the institution of cookery in France by developing codifications that appeared in cook books (Ferguson, 1998), Sade sought to change sexual behaviour by developing his recipes for extreme sexual feats.

Perhaps the most immediately striking feature of Sade's recommendations is their excessive nature. They rarely involve a simple scene of a couple copulating. Rather they typically involve excessively crude, violent and cruel acts. A typical page of Sade's writing will involve the unusual use of semen, anal sex, group sex, restriction of freedom through restraint, rape, threats to life, paedophilia and murder. These acts are typically performed by large teams of well-trained participants and involve complicated combinations of bodies. We quickly become aware that Sade is in no way attempting to spin an erotic tale. Within seconds of setting eyes upon Sade's work, we are plunged into a cruel and perverted world which unreasonably exceeds any apparent moral order. Indeed the events are so disgusting that they defy our imagination. Then, once Sade has shocked us beyond belief, he simply keeps on going, *ad nauseum*. He piles one obscene fantasy upon another. The end result is the sexual version of the complex architectural dishes produced by post-revolutionary French chefs such as Carême and his followers (Mennell, 1985: 144–57). What Sade presents us with is an array of excessively complex, highly organised examples of sexual behaviour. Indeed, 'there is nothing haphazard in Sadean torture' (Frappier-Mazur, 1998: 187). Rather, all sexual acts are meticulously organised and ordered. All details are given by the precise number of people involved, the positioning of various limbs, the equipment which is required, how the victims should undress, even the peculiar knots to be used. According to Adorno and Horkheimer (1972: 88) this reflects the extreme push to administer even the most intimate aspects of human life with little concern for the substantive outcome. Sade radicalises the same desire to administer and regulate sexual activity that we found amongst the medical fraternity, the educationalists and the demographers. Instead of seeking to reignite the flame of passion in sexual life, he tries to ensure that the orgies are excessively organised.

Hiding behind the fornication, then, is a strict regulatory scheme. We notice that in many of his works Sade systematically numbers each act. For instance, *The 120 Days of Sodom* strictly catalogues and lists the extreme acts that are described. What we are presented with is a kind of carefully prepared shopping list of sexual extremism. It seems that these numbers are designed for easy cataloguing and consultation by the literary critic. Indeed, even within reports of Sade's earlier sexual antics accountancy seems to play a central role. In one instance in his earlier years, 'he had himself whipped, but every couple of minutes he would dash to the mantelpiece and, with a knife, would inscribe on the chimney flue the number of lashes he had just received' (de Beauvoir, 1966: 27). This hyper-rational framework seems strange given the fact that such extreme acts are being described. Here we perhaps should note Foucault's condemnation of Sade: 'he bores us. He's a disciplinarian, a sargent of sex, an accountant of the ass and its equivalents' (Foucault, 1996: 186). Similarly, Deleuze comments that 'Rationalism is not grafted onto the work of Sade; it is rather by an internal necessity that he evolves the idea of a delusion, an exorbitance specific to reason' (1991: 27). This reminds us how Sade attempts to rationalise and calculate even the most outlandish sexual acts. It seems that Sade does not take the pleasure from the act itself. Instead, he seems to enjoy fitting them into a neatly ordered balance sheet. Not only does he provide us with a carefully organised apparatus for undertaking wild sexuality, but this apparatus is carefully accounted for.

Part of this desire to account for sexual acts is Sade's desire to detail every possible kind of sexual act. One of the most excessive things about Sade's work is his willingness and desire to 'say everything'. For Sade 'the first of all freedoms is the freedom to say everything. That is how he interpreted the basic requirement – in the form of a demand which, for him, was henceforth inseparable from a true republic' (Blanchot, 1967: 50). He takes this demand of the republic for everything to be said and brought out into public discourse to the extreme. Even the crudest of sexual acts should not be passed over in silence. Rather, it should be allowed to appear in public discourse. According to some commentators (Blanchot, 1967; Keenan, 1998), this points to a deeper political commitment to a kind of radical republicanism whereby Sade sought to take seriously the promises of the revolution. In particular, we notice that Sade attempts to take seriously the claim for liberty and saw this as only achievable through a consistent and thorough-going process of republicanism. Sade

> says that to be a republican it is not enough to live in a republic; nor is a constitution enough to make a republic; nor, finally, is having laws enough for that creative power, that constituent act, to resist and keep us in a state of permanent constitution. An effort must be made, yet another effort, always – there lies the invisible irony. Whence the conclusion – barely hinted at – that the revolutionary era is just beginning. But what kind of effort will have to be made? Who will ask us to make it? Sade calls it *insurrection*, which is *the permanent state of the republic*. In other words the republic can never possibly be a state, but only a movement. (Blanchot, 1967: 53)

By taking the claim to liberty seriously, it appears that the demand that Sade puts forth is not only for the ability to unsettle the institutions which regulate sexuality and impose a new set of more rational and organised ones. Rather, Sade demanded a continued state of change and flux around sexuality. He did this by advocating a continued unsettling of any established forms. Through his extreme shock-tactics, Sade sought to so unsettle the dominant discourse that it would be impossible for it to be re-anchored. He aimed to create a permanent movement in sexualities rather than an institutional freezing. This movement would be akin to the gale of creative destruction the entrepreneur consistently blows up (Schumpeter, 1944: 81–86). This is a demand for what we might call 'positive freedom' that involves not just the demand not to be interfered with by others (see Berlin, 1969), but the recognition that laws are made by humans and that we are able to re-create laws for ourselves (Keenan, 1998). This involves a demand for the ability to continually create new rules and laws around sexuality and have these rules applied to our own sexual behaviour. More than anything, Sade seems to demand absolute freedom in which any combination and constitution of sexuality becomes possible.

Taking seriously this call to absolute freedom results in possibly the most striking aspect of Sade's text – the existence of untrammelled violence. Indeed, for some literary critics the central aspect of Sade's writings is precisely this violence (Frappier-Mazur, 1996). We should be clear that the kind of violence which we find in Sade is not the kind of violence committed in the heat of passion, which subsides when the attendant passion ebbs. Rather, it is a kind of coldly and rationally executed violence. According to de Beauvoir 'he never for an instant loses himself in his animal nature; he remains so lucid, so cerebral, that philosophical discourse, far from depleting his ardour, acts as an aphrodisiac' (1966: 21). Indeed in many of the lengthy philosophical dialogues which punctuate the orgies in Sade's work, we find that his characters are simply taking the demands of the revolution at its word and demand absolute liberty. They seek to justify their acts to themselves in the terms of liberty and sovereignty. Sade demands a kind of unconditional sovereignty – the ability to decide for oneself, without any external interference. Indeed he rejects all submission to any externally imposed strictures and opts for a stringent sovereignty of the individual.

> Sade said over and over again in different ways that we are born alone, there are no links between one man and another. The only rule of conduct then is that I prefer those things which affect me pleasurably and set at nought the undesirable effects of my preferences on other people. The greatest suffering of others always counts for less than my own pleasure. What matter if I must purchase my most trivial satisfaction through a fantastic accumulation of wrong-doing? For my satisfaction gives me pleasure, it exists in myself, but the consequences of the crime do not touch me, they are outside me. (Blanchot cited in Bataille, 2001: 168)

What Blanchot makes us all too aware of here is how Sade pushes the logic of liberty and individual sovereignty to the extreme. Sade's own sexual pleasures are the only thing considered. This means that any violence visited against others is simply a trivial means to the greater and more rationally sustained end of individual liberty, and in this case the liberty to enjoy. This radical individual liberty results in violence and pain being routinely inflicted upon others. Indeed, by taking the liberty of others through turning them into objects for satisfying his own pleasures, Sade seeks to add to his own liberty, his own sovereignty. Little matter if this involves the violent disregard of the other's wants and needs, or if it ends with the extermination of the other through the most extreme and horrific means.

This pure drive towards sexual liberty with absolutely no regard for the others involved reminds us that Sade's heroes remain terminally closed. They are condemned to have a pathological self-interest. Indeed, it has been noted that Sade suffered a kind of autism, and that this 'prevented him from ever forgetting himself or being genuinely aware of the reality of the other person' (de Beauvoir, 1966: 23). Sade's libertines are not in any way able to open themselves up to the other people that they sexually engage with. Instead the other is reduced to a mere object who must be transcended. Because they are unable to recognise the other, they show no capacity for shame. Any act they undertake is not considered to be shameful because there is no-one they recognise in order to be ashamed in front of. Second, because they cannot recognise the other, there is no possibility for an equality of enjoyment. Instead, enjoyment is something which must be jealously guarded. It is not something which can be shared. The Sadean does not engage in moments of swooning of abandon. They are always in possession of themselves and never possessed by others. Indeed, we find that de Beauvoir notes that for Sade 'any enjoyment is mechanical enjoyment when shared' (1966: 33, 35).

Because the Sadean is not able to recognise the other, they are also not able to express remorse to the other. Nor are they able to abandon themselves to loving another person. Rather, loving another person is seen as the utter failure and opposite of what it means to be a libertine. This is because by loving we not only recognise that there is another, but also that the other has a decisive power over us. To love is to diminish one's ability to coldly and rationally control, and this is to escape the Sadean power game (Cusset, 1998). This inability to recognise the other means that Sade's failures are met with a kind of self-obsessed sulking: 'When faced with adversity, he would whine and get upset and become completely distraught' (de Beauvoir, 1966: 9). Ultimately what this shows is that the Sadean has a fear of commonality. Indeed, de Beauvoir (1966:

4) points out that what is so striking about Sade is the fact that he is trying to communicate that which is incommunicable, the impossibility of communication. He is writing about a world where we do not recognise the other, let alone attempt to communicate with them. We just give them orders.

WHY SADE IS NOT AN ENTREPRENEUR

If anything, Sade's efforts to reframe sexuality during the revolution were extreme. We find within his literary output a significant break from the sexual institutions of his day. He seems to have picked up many of the efforts of institutional reform which exploded during the revolution and ruthlessly applied them to sexuality. He followed the revolutionary injunction to replace what were considered to be institutions founded upon superstitions. In their place he sought to erect rationally devised and highly ordered sexual systems. This is notable in his obsession with highly organised mass sexual pursuits and his attempts to maintain a strict accounting regime around these acts. This relentless drive toward the rational and utopian organisation of social systems found in Sade is also found in many of the other efforts of institutional entrepreneurship which appeared following the revolution. Sade also seems to take seriously the espoused goals of liberty and individual sovereignty associated with the revolution. In fact, he takes this claim to liberty to its logical extreme by advocating an absolute liberation of sexuality and the extreme sovereignty of the individual to pursue their sexual pleasure. In doing so he shows how this desire for sovereignty results in an absolute disregard for other people. Indeed, others simply become objects to be given orders and dominated. This unflinching attitude inevitably terminates in the cruel and bloody orgies that appear in his work. We propose that there are at least three reasons why Sade cannot be seen as an entrepreneur, which, to put it very simply, relate to his failure, his place in relation to economics and his ethics.

Sade's attempts to reconstruct the institution of sexuality obviously failed. But why did a libertine such as Sade fail as an institutional entrepreneur when other characters such as the demographers, medics, and educators succeeded? The first and perhaps most obvious answer is that Sade's project was only ever destined to fail. Perhaps his literary output was simply an attempt to imagine an alternative sexual institution rather than a serious attempt to reform existing institutions. Indeed, Sade's own personal debauchery was mild and comparatively limited when compared to the outlandish acts described in his books. Even when he was in a position of power, he did not make any serious efforts to push for sexual reform of the kind suggested by his literary works. It therefore appears that his writing was first and foremost a matter of saying what might happen. It was about taking pleasure in the description rather than in the act which was so central to Sade's efforts. Indeed, 'It was by means of his imagination that he escaped from space, time, prison, and the police, the void of absence, opaque presences, the conflict of existence, death, life, and all contradictions. It was not murder that fulfilled Sade's erotic nature: it was literature' (de Beauvoir, 1966: 33). The only kinds of interventions which Sade therefore intended were interventions into the imagination. He certainly may have achieved a profound change and self-recognition in this sense (Bataille, 2001), but nonetheless he was not able to materialise these flights of fancy. Unlike the medic he was not able to establish clinics, training courses, public events and so on. He certainly imagined these establishments in his books (an erotic education for instance), but no serious efforts were made to construct these institutions. Therefore, the first reason that Sade failed as an entrepreneur was that he was not able to materialise his imaginary world.

Perhaps one of the central reasons that Sade was not able to materialise his narratives was that he did not have access to the economic resources which were required. This was largely because of Sade's place in economic relations as part of the declining aristocracy. To be clear he was not a successful business person, which is to say, he was not *economically* successful – in fact he was an economic disaster. This might remind us that when we appraise entrepreneurship we should never forget that entrepreneurship is an economic category. There has been a widespread tendency to treat the entrepreneur as anything but an economic category, and contemporary readings of entrepreneurship as part of a network of social relations seem to further exacerbate the problem. When entrepreneurs are presented in the media and television, for example, there is a persistent fascination in their seemingly unique personality, lifestyle, or individual foibles – anything but their economic calculations. This is mirrored in entrepreneurship research, which equally seems to both assume and disavow the place of economics in the designation of the category of 'entrepreneurship'. This is a direct correlation, although in inverted form, of the problem of commodity fetishism. While commodity fetishism, following Marx, involves 'a definite social relation between men, that assumes, in their eyes, the fantastic form of a relation between things' (1954: 77), in contemporary social analysis today we find exactly the opposite: the treatment of relations between things in the fantastic form of a relation between people. Thus Žižek calls on the need to reverse Marx's formula, and argues that:

in contemporary capitalism, *the objective market 'relations between things' tend to assume the phantasmagorical form of pseudo-personalised 'relations between people'*. No, Bill Gates is no genius, good or bad, he is just an opportunist who knew how to seize the moment and, as such, the result of the capitalist system run amok. (1999: 349–50).

Indeed it was Sade's position within the economic structure that allowed him to engage in imaginary flights of fancy but never to materialise them. Unlike the successful institutional entrepreneurs who did manage to reform sexuality, Sade did not have access to the necessary resources to pursue his plans. He was thereby cursed to forever remain in the realms of his own devious imagination.

Third, and perhaps the most obvious reason that Sade is not widely placed within the pantheon of entrepreneurs, is that he was ethically repugnant. But if we are to dismiss Sade on moral criteria, we need to be quite clear about why it is that Sade is indeed so ethically objectionable. Certainly he violates just about every common law that Western societies possess (rape, murder, paedophilia, to name but a few). However, what is it that is the deeper ethical lack which we so abhor about Sade's behaviour? For us, the abhorrence we feel is because, at the heart of Sade, is his patent inability and even unwillingness to recognise the other. That is, his drive towards absolute self-sovereignty is done in utter disregard of the other person. Indeed, as we have seen, Sade assumed that to be utterly sovereign, the pains of the other must be completely disregarded. They are only important to the extent that they increased Sade's own enjoyment. This of course violates perhaps one of the central ethical maxims – 'love thy neighbour' (see Žižek et al., 2006). Sade seems intent on establishing an absolutely negative relationship with other people (Klossowski, 1966: 69). By establishing this negative relationship he seems to focus on absolutely obliterating the wishes of the other. It is from this attitude that many of the cruel acts described within Sade's work flow. Following this, we suggest that Sade is unethical because he is not able to recognise the other.

WHO IS AN ENTREPRENEUR?

The case of Sade today might seem like a museum piece of the horrors of revolutionary excesses. However, he offers the study of entrepreneurship some profound lessons. First and foremost he reminds us that entrepreneurship is not something simply limited to the astute businessman. His efforts to imagine other worlds are certainly entrepreneurial, even if they did, and should, fail. Second, with the case of Sade we find the aspects which are central to contemporary entrepreneurship taken to their logical extreme. For instance, we find that a commitment to individual liberty and absolute sovereignty is taken to its logical and disturbing extremes. Sade gives us an indication of what the dire consequences would be of a world ruled only by the logic of utter and unflinching self-interest. Critically, many entrepreneurs, and many entrepreneurship researchers, have explicitly or implicitly assumed exactly the same concept of self-interest that we find in the Marquis de Sade. Finally, Sade's own failures provide us with an indication of some of the other disregarded characteristics which an entrepreneur must have – that is the ability to materialise their inventions, with access to necessary resources to do so, and finally of being considered at least minimally ethical – that is, being able to recognise and account for the needs and desires of the other. Perhaps it is by heeding these warnings that we can unmask common understandings of entrepreneurship and construct more ethically sensitive accounts of the politics of entrepreneurship.

But this will require us to take very seriously the challenge that cases such as Sade present to entrepreneurship discourse, as it normally operates. We are concerned here with a recent tendency to make efforts to 'soften' entrepreneurship discourse, to expand it so as to cover almost any form of social or institutional innovation (Steyaert and Hjorth, 2006). One of the reasons that Sade is important is because, when accounting for social and institutional innovations, the question that is often lurking in the background, unstated and unanalysed, is the question of the 'goodness' of that social innovation. In many of the cases of proposed social entrepreneurship, there is an implicit coding of social entrepreneurship as progressive, socially purposeful, and good. With Sade, it is much harder to find such a code, although we should remember that Sade saw himself as a moral philosopher and as a progressive.

This lack of an account of ethics is one of the fatal failings of current work on social and institutional entrepreneurship. It tends to make social and institutional innovation into instrumental matters, so that we can then know *how to do it*, when in fact many actors involved in social and institutional innovation are actively concerned about *why* they are seeking to change social institutions. Obviously we need to know how to change things, but we also need a space to open up the conversation about why we might change things, and in which directions. At present this is lacking in social and institutional entrepreneurship research. Entrepreneurship discourse unfortunately tends to share with Sade a certain 'autism', that is, it focuses on the entrepreneur doing the innovating and is largely uninterested in those who collaborate with the entrepreneur, and those others for whom innovation is proposed.

In an important paper published in 1989, Bill Gartner proposed that the question 'Who is an entrepreneur?' is the wrong question. That paper offered a very important critique of theories of entrepreneurship that assumed that the principal question of entrepreneurship was to identify the traits of this or that entrepreneur. In this chapter, based on our analysis of the Marquis de Sade, we argue that there is a very different way in which one can put the question 'Who is an entrepreneur?'. Put in a different way, and with attention to the exclusions of entrepreneurship discourse, it could be that 'who is an entrepreneur' might exactly be the *right* question. This is not to say that we need some return to trait theories of entrepreneurship. Rather, it is to say that by considering carefully those to whom the category of entrepreneurship is and is not applied, we can learn a great deal about the inclusions and exclusions of entrepreneurship discourse, and about its assumed moral and political grounds.

These inclusions and exclusions are too important to be ignored. The economic and cultural stakes are too high. We have tried to account for these stakes in Chapters 4 and 5, in terms of the attribution of value to particular actors, and the related attribution of financial benefits. Here we might have added one or two layers to those analyses by drawing attention to the implicit moral and political grounding of entrepreneurship studies, and the value judgements that they necessarily entail. Beginning to account for, and to critically scrutinise, those moral and political judgements, is one of the pressing tasks before us today. This might begin to take us beyond the moral prejudices and political exclusions that are today the mark of talk of the entrepreneur. We will return to the question of the moral valuation of the entrepreneur in Chapter 8, but we will first consider another instance of what might seem to be unlikely entrepreneurship.

7. Every age gets the entrepreneur it deserves

There is one thing we know about entrepreneurs to be sure – the entrepreneur is an ambiguous, uncertain, and paradoxical character who evades most attempts at capture. So far in this book, we have argued that such ambiguity is an important feature of entrepreneurship discourse. Indeed, it is this ambiguity that makes the entrepreneur such an alluring and omnipresent figure, another result being that the boundaries of what is and is not entrepreneurship are actually quite difficult to discern. In the previous chapter we looked at the enterprising behaviours of one of the most unlikely entrepreneurs one could imagine, the Marquis de Sade. We argued that a shocking figure like Sade reminds us that there are certain boundaries to who can be called an entrepreneur.

But it is not just unlikely entrepreneurs such as Sade who are excluded from 'being entrepreneurial'. There are many other figures that haunt the contemporary economy who appear to be very entrepreneurial, but are not likely to gain the title of being an entrepreneur. These are often shadowy figures who lurk in the grey or black economy. They include people working without declaring their income, illegal workers, gamblers, small-time thieves, street hustlers, pornographers, arms dealers, forgers, prostitutes, drug dealers, and organised criminals of various kinds. These characters engage in what is highly entrepreneurial behaviour, that is, they find and create markets, they take risks, they perceive opportunities, they undertake business ventures (see Williams, 2006; Volkov, 2002). Semi-legal street traders in New York engaged in entrepreneurial behaviour to create a new market for used magazines, although they were denied the status of being entrepreneurs, rendering their activities illegal and highly precarious (Durier, 1999). Women in poor Chicago neighbourhoods engaged in a whole range of illegal and semi-legal jobs such as using their car as an illegal 'gypsy cab', cooking soul food and selling it to local businesses, or holding illegal gambling parties (Venkatesh, 2006).

In such cases, the homeless New Yorkers and poor residents of Chicago are highly entrepreneurial. However, they are not normally recognised as 'entrepreneurs'. This was because these people were not able to able to access the status, respect and additional claims on economic value that come with being an entrepreneur. In an analogous way, Bent Meier Sørensen has forcefully argued that the figure of the entrepreneur is best represented in the genuinely creative acts of, for example, St Paul, or a naked performance artist taking a bath in urine-infused milk (see Sørensen, 2008, 2009). The central problem we find here is not that the discourse of entrepreneurship is too all-encompassing and has embraced these apparently marginal characters. Rather, the problem is that each of these characters cannot be identified or even thought about as an entrepreneur. They are merely thought about as 'bottom feeders' lurking in the depths of the 'grey economy'.

It is surprising that these figures rarely surface in accounts of entrepreneurship, because this underground economy is huge. It is estimated to make up 9 per cent of the United States economy (McTague, 2005; for other estimates see Lippert and Walker, 1997; National Centre for Policy Analysis, 1998; US Department of Labor, 1992). As well as hiding a significant sector of the economy, it also disqualifies many people who do all the things that entrepreneurs are supposed to do (such as coming up with innovative combinations of the means of production) but who do not fit into the confines of being a successful business person. This renders us blind to all the 'shady' forms of entrepreneurship that go on in contemporary economies. This blindness means that we make ourselves largely ignorant of a rapidly growing and vibrant sector of economic life.

In this chapter, we would like to go some way to unmask some of these tidy prejudices about entrepreneurship. We take as our starting point recent research that recognises that entrepreneurship thrives in the 'shady' economy. In particular we will ask how it is that these characters are usually excluded from being called entrepreneurs. We are interested in what specific processes of exclusion are involved. By looking at these, we hope to address the broader question of what this tells us about the culture of enterprise and entrepreneurship more generally. We address each of these questions by focusing on one character in contemporary society who is systematically denied access to the title of 'entrepreneur'. This is the illegal immigrant. We focus on this figure because it brings to light many aspects associated with entrepreneurship such as risk taking and recognising and exploiting opportunities (Shane, 2000, 2003). But despite the fact that illegal immigrants formally comply with these characteristics, they remain unable to claim the status of being entrepreneurs. We ask why this is.

In order to answer this question, we look at a particularly tragic case of illegal immigrant labour that was revealed by the death of 23 Chinese nationals who were collecting cockles on the sands of Morecambe Bay in North West England during 2004. This case is particularly interesting because it is a clear instance of the 'dark side' of entrepreneurship that confronts us with shocking and visceral realities (cf. Kets de Vries, 1985). It reminds us that entrepreneurship does not just involve stories of success, but also often grim and sometimes deadly examples of failure. Second, it is a theoretically interesting case because the people working on the sands of Morecambe Bay on that day were engaged in many of the activities identified by entrepreneurship research, but were not considered to be proper entrepreneurs. By selecting a case that should conform with current theories but does not we are able to capture some of the limitations of current theories of entrepreneurship. Finally, the case also provoked a considerable outpouring of discussion, debate and investigation around the topic of illegal immigration, both in the press and in society more broadly.

WELCOME TO MORECAMBE BAY

On the morning of 5 February 2004, a group of Chinese nationals living in Liverpool were collected by a driver in a mini-van. They were then driven over an hour to Morecambe Bay on the North West coast of England. Morecambe Bay is well known for having particularly treacherous tides and rapidly shifting sands, and is home to many cockles, a small shell-fish that is eaten throughout Europe. These cockles can be collected for sale if one possesses a licence. The Chinese nationals would be driven out onto the sands. They would then proceed to collect and bag cockles during the day and would be paid for each bag collected. These bags would then be sold on to fishery companies in Liverpool who would, in turn, sell the cockles to Dutch suppliers.

As evening approached, the Morecambe Bay tide began to rise. This was barely perceptible to the cockle-pickers at first. However once the tide began rising it rapidly picked up pace. At this point the cockle-pickers began to panic. A series of mobile phone calls were made to their employer, to the emergency services, and to their families back in China. Rescue services were dispatched at about 9 pm. They were only able to recover six of the cockle-pickers. A handful of others had made their way to the shore earlier. However an uncertain number were still missing in the waters of Morecambe Bay.

In the following days, 21 bodies of drowned cockle-pickers were recovered. Two other bodies were never found. A large-scale police investigation was launched, which revealed that most of the cockle-pickers were from the Fujian province of China. Most were also working without appropriate legal documentation. Many of the cockle-pickers had entered the country illegally with the help of so-called 'snake-head gangs'. The investigations also revealed that the people who had organised the cockle-picking venture were Lin Liangren, who had established the operation, his girl-friend Zhao Xiao Qing, and his cousin Lin Mu Yong. The cockles were to be supplied to a Liverpool-based seafood company run by the father-and-son team of David and Tony Eden.

The death of the 23 cockle-pickers sparked a national debate about the role of undocumented workers in the United Kingdom. This included reflection on the role they play in the economy, legislation around immigrant workers, conditions of employment for them, policing of immigrant workers, and living conditions of some them. At the heart of these debates was the concern that the death of these 23 people was the result of entrepreneurialism going too far. In what follows we shall trace out this debate.

THE COCKLE-PICKERS

Perhaps the dominant way of describing the cockle-pickers was as 'illegals'. Indeed, the immigration status of the cockle-pickers was inevitably the first thing which many media reports noted. In some texts their immigration status was given as a simple fact: 'most were illegal immigrants or asylum seekers' (Tozer, 2004: 6). As on other occasions we find that the cockle-pickers were one of many in a large surge of immigrants who had followed a 'well-trodden path'. As one early report noted, as information about the deaths came in:

> Many of the 19 Chinese cockle pickers who drowned in Morecambe Bay were believed to have been illegal immigrants. Some are thought to have arrived in Europe on tourist visas before being smuggled into Britain. Group tours in particular have been used to fly would-be illegal immigrants to Eastern Europe, from where they follow a well-trodden path to Britain. (Spencer, 2004: 7)

Indeed, a number of people linked these cocklers with what they perceived to be widespread failures in the asylum system. For these commentators, the cockle-pickers were evidence of the failures in the British asylum system:

> Today Britain is home to four million immigrants, many illegal and unknown. The Government hasn't a clue exactly how many – and wouldn't tell us if it did. Who cares? The economy is booming. But so is violent crime, pressure on scarce housing, schools and hospital care. Aids and TB cases, mostly imported, are spiralling upwards. London is bursting at the seams. Even today, two years

> after Morecambe Bay, illegal immigrants are slaving for wages in conditions no
> British union would tolerate. (Kavanagh, 2006)

In this passage we find the cockle-pickers represented as illegals, but precisely what the implications are of their immigration status is changed
significantly. For some it is a stated fact, for others it is evidence of the
continued 'flood' of immigrants into the UK.

The cockle-pickers were also represented as figures who were supporting impoverished families in China. One Chinese worker interviewed in
connection with the tragedy said 'I am in Britain because I want my six-
year-old son in China to have a better life' (Harvey, 2004). Others are said
to be working to support entire families in poor villages. For instance,
one newspaper report of a village from which one of the dead cockle-
pickers came was described as being supported by sons and daughters who
worked overseas:

> Baihu is among the most squalid places in China – a village of rutted roads,
> dank housing and washing lines filled with torn children's clothing. It is a
> place the Chinese economic miracle has passed by. Since the closure of several
> factories in the 1990s, locals estimate the unemployment rate to be over 50%.
> Most families, they say, depend on a son or a daughter who is working illegally
> overseas. (Watts, 2004: 9)

Indeed, stories of familial financial hardship and economic disaster were
often used to explain what drove the cockle-pickers to their doom. Stories
were told of some of the cockle-pickers' families, who had entered into
ventures such as farming or fisheries only to have their livelihood crushed
by a freak storm or the changing agricultural market. Other less salubri-
ous motives for working illegally abroad were also noted in the press.
This included funding the building of large 'Spanish villas' (Kennedy et
al., 2004: 11) for family members in their home villages. Not withstanding
these different motives for seeking out employment in the UK, the cockle-
pickers were all represented as people who had been cruelly separated
from their families. Perhaps the most heart-wrenching examples of these
close ties can be found in stories of panicked phone calls from the cocklers
to their families in China as the tide rose:

> Others made frantic mobile phone calls to relatives in China, bidding an
> anguished farewell with their dying breaths. 'I am in great danger,' father-of-
> two Guo Bing Long, 28 told his wife in Fujian Province, more than 6,000 miles
> away. 'I am up to my chest in water. Maybe I am going to die.' Then, as the
> water rose, Mr Long, who, like most of the victims was a Christian, said: 'Tell
> the family to pray for me. It's too close. I am dying.' (Craven and Tozer, 2006:
> 4)

Putting aside the horrific scene painted here, what is interesting is how the cocklers are positioned not just as self-serving 'illegals', but as members of a broader family who depend on their labours and willingness to take great risks and travel to the other side of the world in search of work.

Another frequent way that the cockle-pickers appeared in the press were as people who lacked the crucial 'local knowledge' required to engage in cockle-picking on the sands of Morecambe Bay. This lack of knowledge made them clearly unable to deal with the difficult conditions they were working in:

> Alan Archer, 35, a local farmer, went out to the cockle beds at 6 am and spent more than four hours gathering 11 [eleven] 40 kg bags of shellfish. 'You have to know where the right spots are,' he said. 'There was not a lot of talk about the Chinese today. All that had gone on before. They just didn't have the vehicles or the gear to get off the sands safely.' Alan Griffiths, 46, who uses the global positioning system to help him fish the beds in safety, will be out on the sands today. 'We had given up on the job on the Thursday of the tragedy,' he said. 'There was only about a tonne of cockles there on the Wednesday because we lost an hour each way as the tide came in. But the Chinese kept going. One of their Land Rovers is still out there. They did not learn the lesson'. (Ward and Watts, 2004: 11)

There was frequent mention in the press of how locals had left the sands earlier in the day, and in some cases had warned the Chinese cockle-pickers of the rising tide. Indeed the cockle-pickers were represented as being in some cases wholly unskilled for the task of cockle-picking as 'Most were from farming backgrounds. Some could swim and others could not. Some had never seen the sea before heading for Britain' (Bunyan, 2006: 4), and they were 'unable to speak sufficient English to summon help' (Bunyan, 2005: 13). This complete lack of experience and knowledge portrays the cocklers as people who were undertaking a task which was wholly inappropriate for them. Their deaths were partially due to their lack of skills needed for working the sands at Morecambe Bay.

Throughout the media reporting, we find that the cockle-pickers were also frequently represented as being victims. Perhaps the most notable image of victimhood we can find is the frequent reference to their position as slaves. For instance, the cockle-pickers were represented as people who suffered a fate of human bondage:

> Drowning in the icy waters of Morecambe Bay was an avoidable catastrophe. But it was the inevitable consequence of policies that gave organised crime the green light for people smuggling. Human bondage is hugely profitable. It rakes in billions and is less risky than drugs. Desperate men and women of all races and religions pay dearly for their one way ticket to Europe – with Britain the destination of choice. (Kavanagh, 2006)

If the cockle-pickers are slaves, we must ask ourselves who they are slaves to? The answer we find in the press is two-fold. Perhaps the most visible face of the slave-master we find is a brutal combination of snake-head gangs and local Chinese gang-masters: 'Many of these immigrants are heavily in debt to snakehead gangs and must take the first job they can find to clear the money they borrowed to get here' (Lawrence et al., 2004: 1). This indebtedness is said to put them in a position where they must pay back the snake-heads through working in menial and sometimes danger-ous jobs. Other accounts try to position the actions of the snake-heads as a manifestation of a far deeper issue of the relationship of victimisation. For these commentators, the cockle-pickers were victims of multinational capitalism. For instance, the cocklers were represented as victims of falling agricultural prices in their home markets, victims of the increasing demand for cheap food in Europe, victims of a new business model of flex-ible employment and short-term contracts, and victims of global inequity. These projected causes are nicely summed up by one newspaper report which declared that 'Drowning will be the word on their death certificate, but it is cowboy capitalism that has caused this dreadful human tragedy' (Woodley, 2004: 22).

This sense of pity is redoubled in texts that position the cocklers as wretches who are living and working in intolerable conditions. Throughout each of the texts, we find frequent descriptions of the extremely poor housing conditions in which these workers lived. Here is one typical description of their living conditions:

> The house's dingy hall leads to the lounge, a room no bigger than two metres square (less than 7ft by 7ft), the largest in this two-storey premises. Here 13 people were watching television. There was no proper furniture, so they sat either on plastic chairs or on the floor against the wall. (Pai, 2004: 4)

The reports on the living conditions of the cocklers emphasised how impoverished their surroundings were. They are frequently referred to as 'slums', 'squalid', or 'cramped'. One report paints a grim picture of 'a stinking communal lavatory and a small pot-strewn kitchen' (Harvey, 2004). The numbers of people living in each house varies wildly from about ten up to sixty. One newspaper even goes as far as claiming 'They sleep using their cockle sacks as hammocks and are even said to bed down in graveyards' (*Sun*, 2004).

The conditions under which the cocklers worked are represented as being just as horrific. Their massively sub-standard wages are called to our attention: 'these people were being paid one fifth of the standard rate for their work' (Chapman and Tozer, 2004: 4). The wages they received were estimated as being anything from £1 to £10 per day. Equally shocking were the extremely poor standards of safety under which they worked. For instance, one experienced cockle-picker commented:

> Back in March and April it was absolutely freezing and those poor souls were wading in with no wellies, no waterproofs, no warm clothing and no lifejackets – it was a tragedy waiting to happen. I thought that if somebody drowned I wouldn't be able to live with myself and I tried to put a stop to it, but they just wouldn't listen. (Chapman and Tozer, 2004: 4)

The difficult and arduous conditions of work are also noted by one news-paper in an interview with a cockle-picker: 'The work is very hard. It is cold and hurts my back. I don't even know when and how much I'll get paid. I'm depressed. I want to quit, but I have no freedom, no choice because I'm illegal' (*Guardian*, 2004: 2). In each of these passages, one can see a picture of the cockle-pickers as people who are forced to live in sub-human conditions and work in dangerous situations for little or no pay.

The final way that we find the cockle-pickers represented in the press is as hardworking and aspirational characters. Instead of being victims of fate, the workers are 'incredibly hard working, sending money back to their families. They were also astute. They had come to Britain because the exchange rate was high and they liked the "kind and polite" people' (Thomson, 2004: 26). They take up 'the menial jobs that we refuse to do any more – washing up, cleaning, mini cab driving, factory work, construction, textiles, agricultural work and, increasingly, nursing and teaching' (Thomson, 2004: 26).

Indeed they are represented as characters who will seize any opportu-nity available: 'Obviously any job the British don't want to do, the Chinese will do it. Chinese don't look down on any job if they can get money and feed their family. This is their attitude' (Kennedy et al., 2004: 11). Indeed these opportunities are even seized in the black market economy which has 'been greedily swallowing up the Fujianese who cannot get proper work. Some sell bootleg DVDs on the streets. Some become prostitutes . . . Picking shellfish is the latest job opportunity' (Kennedy et al., 2004: 11). Their move to the UK to work in these jobs was not just seen as the result of being duped by snake-head gangs. Rather it was a somewhat considered move made by people who sought to take what they realised would be a significant risk in order to make their fortunes abroad. Some compare the state of life in China to what is available in Britain: 'In China', he said 'life was not too good . . . we want to come to Britain because you can earn good money. Life is good there' (Lawrence et al., 2004: 1). In other cases, their temporary suffering is represented as one step towards better opportunities. For instance one Chinese worker interviewed by a newspaper stated: 'I want to stay in Britain forever. I would like to open a Chinese takeaway. There are lots of jobs and opportunities here' (Harvey, 2004). These dreams of success abroad are spurred on by tales in local villages of immigrants who had managed to become hugely successful abroad and plough money back into their local communities:

> 'My son in England built us this', says a proud mother, showing visitors around a newly completed six-storey building – the tallest in a nearby village – complete with pillars, balconies and stucco decorations. 'It costs 500,000 renminbi, but he can afford it because he has a good job: he works in a bakery.' The son sends back about 10,000 renminbi per month (about 700 pounds) – more than 10 times what a local worker would earn. The baker-prince has lifted the family out of poverty by going overseas. (*Guardian*, 2004: 2)

Here we find that by seizing the opportunity of working in an apparently 'menial' job, the son has been able to create large gains for his family and show the benefits of his hardship. This effectively transforms him from being a victim of snake-heads and poor conditions to being an aspirational and entrepreneurial worker.

WERE THEY ENTREPRENEURS?

At first glance, it seems ridiculous to claim that illegal immigrant workers like the Morecambe Bay cockle-pickers could be considered entrepreneurs. Reflecting on the basic 'facts' of the case, we seem to have here a story of labourers working in particularly poor conditions for meagre wages. Indeed the kind of labour process which we found in this case mirrors the findings of many other studies of immigrant labour in Western countries (see, for example, Schlosser, 2003; Soldatenko, 1999). However, when we turn to the representations of the cockle-pickers in public debate a slightly different story emerges. We certainly notice that a common story found in so many other places was woven around the cockle-pickers. They are illegal immigrants who have entered the UK to work in order to support impoverished families. When they arrived they became victims of snake-head gangs, evil gang-masters and the rampant inequities of multinational capitalism. This forced them to take up jobs for which they had very little ability and to live in conditions that were sub-human. This terrible situation led them to their death on the sands of Morecambe Bay. This narrative clearly positions the cockle-pickers as people who suffered at the hands of unscrupulous entrepreneurs rather than as entrepreneurs themselves.

But sitting alongside this picture of the cockle-picker as victim of entrepreneurship is a quite different representation. This is one that represents the cockle-picker as someone who behaves very much like an entrepreneur – willing to take extreme risks, they are aspirational, able to perceive gaps in the English market for cheap agricultural labour and fill them, and able to persevere despite highly adverse conditions. This reminds us of all the 'entrepreneurial' activities that the cockle-pickers were involved in. However, it was also a representation that played only a very minor part in the overall public story of the cockle-pickers. Why such a minor part? Why was it necessary to cleanse these cockle-pickers of the traces of entrepreneurship? To put this question rather bluntly: why were these illegal immigrants disqualified from being considered entrepreneurial?

In this case the one characteristic that the illegal immigrants do not share with 'normal' entrepreneurs is the fact that they were illegal. They were without papers, *sans papiers*, that is, they were without the necessary legal documents to undertake their enterprises within the country. The central thing holding back these cockle-pickers – like most illegal immigrants – from claiming the title of entrepreneur is the law, in particular, immigration law.

If we remained in the shoals of common sense, the exceptional status of the illegal immigrant would not invite any extensive analysis. All that would be required is the identification of the various legal codes that exclude the illegal immigrant and the slight amendment of broad definitions of the entrepreneur as someone who is legally allowed to be in a particular state. However, such a dry manoeuvre would only leave us within the law, and would reveal the specific legal limitations on enterprise. What it would not do is specify the political antagonisms which underlie these curtailments. This would effectively blind us to the fact that the illegal immigrant is not simply excluded by a technical law. Even when legal sanctions around immigration are relaxed, immigrants still remain excluded from societies in a whole range of ways. It therefore seems that these patterns of exclusion are rooted in a far deeper political law that may or may not find expression in formal legislation. We therefore propose to think through this political-symbolic state of exclusion by turning to the work of Carl Schmitt and Giorgio Agamben.

For Schmitt, the law of politics is exception. That is, any properly political situation involves a fundamental, necessary and central exclusion. The figure who must necessarily be excluded by politics is defined as the enemy. For Schmitt, 'the specific political distinction to which political actions and motives can be reduced is that between friend and enemy' (1996: 6). According to Schmitt this vital distinction is irreducible to other criteria such as aesthetics (judgements about beauty and ugliness), ethics (judgements about good and bad), and economics (judgements about profitability and unprofitability). Often an enemy may be a source of profit, may be ethical, and may even be beautiful. Nonetheless they remain an enemy. So, we need to ask, what is it for Schmitt that marks out an enemy? For him, the defining characteristic is that the enemy is 'the other, the stranger; and it is sufficient for his nature that he is, in a specially intense way, existentially something different and alien, so that in extreme cases conflicts with him are possible' (Schmitt, 1996: 27). Schmitt goes further to note that this difference must be an absolute and extreme one if we are to make an enemy out of the other person. This becomes clear when Schmitt points out that the enemy is a public enemy – that is the enemy of the wider group to which we belong. They are not the intimate or private enemy, our neighbour for instance. They are the absolute other to our collective.

With the designation of the enemy as the collective stranger, the position of the illegal immigrant begins to become clear. They are deemed strange, not-like-us. This is reinforced through the constant anti-immigration rhetoric found in the tabloid newspapers and the like. Immigrants might be tolerated if they have made certain efforts to be 'like us'. In this respect they might be allowed to identify themselves as 'migrant entrepreneurs'. However, if they remain without the appropriate papers they remain completely other, and strange. In short, they remain enemies. And because they are outside the public, they cannot lay claim to the various identities that are made available to members of that public. One of these identities of course is the entrepreneur. So instead of claiming the identity of the entrepreneur, they must remain rogue traders.

Schmitt's theory of the enemy reminds us that lurking under all apparently simple legal issues such as the illegality of the entrepreneur is a more profound and indeed disturbing political reality. This is particularly fitting because Schmitt was concerned with what he saw as a fundamental category error made in much liberal political thought of his time which confused or reduced the political to other spheres, such as the moral or the economic. He argues:

> In a very systematic fashion liberal thought evades or ignores state and politics and moves instead in a typical always recurring polarity of two heterogeneous spheres, namely ethics and economics, intellect and trade, education and property. The critical distrust of state and politics is easily explained by the principles of a system whereby the individual must remain *terminus a quo* and *terminus ad quem*. (1996: 70–71)

It is precisely this situation that discussion of examples such as the Morecambe Bay disaster is locked into. On the one hand we have the *Economist* (2004) with its infinitely pragmatic assessment of the situation as simply the result of the confluence of a number of economic forces. On the other hand we have the *Daily Telegraph* (Nicolson, 2004) with its allusions to a Turner painting coupled with moral outrage at a situation where poor lost souls were left to perish by feckless gang-masters on the desolate sands of Morecambe Bay. What we do not have in such a debate is explicit reflection on the political constitution that played a part in the death of these 23 people. Such a reflection would at the very least begin with Schmitt's distinctly unsettling question of 'who is our enemy?'. The answer, we would probably be appalled to find, would be that the collective of Britain rendered these enterprising souls as illegals, illegitimates, in short, enemies. By making an 'apolitical' assessment of the situation we forget the (unattractive) antagonisms that deprived these strangers on the Morecambe sands of papers, thereby depriving them of their enterprise, and ultimately, their lives.

STATE OF EXCEPTION

Recognising the role of law in constituting who is and is not an entrepreneur is therefore vital in unmasking the prejudices of entrepreneurship discourse and beginning to account for the vital role of politics in the constitution of enterprise. There is, in short, no entrepreneurship without the state. Next, we can begin to consider what it means to dwell outside the state. What does it mean for these Chinese workers to be rendered as 'illegals'? In order to work through this question we will turn to Agamben's (1998, 2005) analysis of the 'state of exception', which builds on and significantly extends the ideas of Schmitt. Agamben begins his analysis of the state of exception by drawing on Schmitt's famous definition of sovereignty as 'he who decides on the state of exception' (Agamben, 1998: 11). He uses this definition to point out that sovereignty involves the establishment of rules and laws – such as the one which deems the entrepreneur inside or outside a polity – but in order to establish this law they must be able to stand outside the law. That is, the sovereign must be able to suspend the law, to create a state of exception. This reminds us that 'the sovereign stands outside the juridical order and, nevertheless, belongs to it, since it is up to him to decide if the constitution is to be suspended *in toto*' (Schmitt, 1985: 7, cited in Agamben, 1998: 15).

This places the sovereign in a state of exception, that is, they are able to establish a law, but they also have the possibility of stepping outside that law. This exception constitutes the law that it legislates: 'The exception does not only conform to the rule; the rule as such lives off the exception' (Schmitt, 1985: 15; cited in Agamben, 1998: 16). Thus the exceptional nature of the sovereign is the ability to step outside of and not be governed by the law. It is this ability which constitutes law. This suggests that a rule, such as what gets defined as legally constituting entrepreneurship, is established by its limit cases, its suspension, its exception. That is, it is established by characters like the enterprising workers of Morecambe Bay who certainly show many of the traits associated with entrepreneurship, but nonetheless are not legally permitted to be entrepreneurs. They are subject to what Agamben calls a 'ban'.

For Agamben the law is precisely supported by drawing a limit, an outside. This is because it is only through maintaining itself in relationship to its outside, its limit, that a law maintains its force. 'The particular "force" of law consists in this capacity to maintain itself in relation to its exteriority' (1998: 8). For the law of entrepreneurship to work, it must render some potential enterprising characters as an exception, that is, as non-entrepreneurial. This is done through identifying a palpable and concrete outside by defining who is *not* an entrepreneur. Indeed, what is interesting for Agamben here is that there is no rigorously specified law that legislates these characters who are outside. Rather, when people are outside they are legislated as individual cases. This often happens through pure force. Thus the illegal immigrant is not treated as someone who may be codified by and through existing law. Rather, they are a character who must be excluded on an individual basis.

The exception (the illegal immigrant) thus proves the rule (the entrepreneur). However, what is perhaps more interesting is that this exception becomes the norm, that is, it is the group who are excluded from the law (a minority) that actually become a majority who are included in this 'state of exception'. For Agamben, perhaps the best representative of this permanent state of exclusion is represented by figures like the illegal immigrant or refugee:

> Given the by now unstoppable decline of the nation-state and the general corrosion of traditional political-juridical categories, the refugee is perhaps the only thinkable figure for the people of our time . . . we will have to abandon decidedly, without reservation, the fundamental concepts through which we have so far represented the subjects of the political (Man, the citizen and its rights, but also the sovereign people, the worker, and so forth) and build our new political philosophy anew starting from the one and only figure of the refugee. (Agamben, 2000: 16)

What is so striking in this statement by Agamben is that the majority of the contemporary public are actually excluded from that public. This seems to be given at least some support by the fact that those without a legal work status are fast becoming the dominant part of certain sectors of the labour market such as agriculture and cleaning. Some areas of small business such as home service, street trading, sex work, and personal transportation (taxi cabs and so forth) are also becoming increasingly dominated by illegal entrepreneurs. In some developing countries, illegal entrepreneurs make up a large part of the entire small-business sector. Thus, it is not simply a matter of identifying the size of an underground economy as an exceptional phenomenon that stands alongside the official economy (see, for example, Ritter, 1998; Fadahunsi and Rosa, 2002; Adis and van Praag, 2007). Rather, it becomes a matter of recognising that this underground is actually at the heart of major parts of the official economy. The result is that 'the exception everywhere becomes the rule' (Agamben, 1998: 9). The exceptional enterprise of characters like the cockle-pickers actually becomes the new rule. The excluded enterprise of many begins to lie at the heart of entrepreneurial efforts. But at the same time it is deemed permanently external to enterprise. The cockle-pickers are therefore the entrepreneurs who cannot and must not be recognised as such. For if they are, the constitutive exception at the heart of the politico-symbolic law of entrepreneurship would be called into question. If these cockle-pickers were to be considered entrepreneurs, it would become far less self-evident who actually was an entrepreneur. This would make it all the more difficult for contemporary culture to lionise the figure of the entrepreneur as well as award it inordinate 'entrepreneurial profits'.

THE LAW OF ENTREPRENEURSHIP

Now we are at a point where we can answer the question we have set ourselves: why are characters like cockle-pickers not considered entrepreneurs? We have argued that despite an apparent correspondence with the characteristics of an entrepreneur, the illegal immigrant is still not deemed to be an entrepreneur. This is fundamentally a question of law. We have seen that illegal immigrants are both excluded through formal juridical law by a deeper political logic. This exclusion is based on the deeper political logic of the friend/enemy distinction. Further, what is of vital importance is that this exclusion is not only interesting as a minor or fringe case. Rather, by being excluded it gives force to the existing law of entrepreneurship. It is the exclusion of characters like the Marquis de Sade and the illegal immigrant that makes the category of the entrepreneur work.

This argument therefore has important consequences. First, it reminds us that the question of who gets to lay claim to the status of being an entrepreneur is not simply a matter of correspondence with formal models. Rather, the identity of the entrepreneur is linked to questions of law. Here we mean law in two senses. First, in the more narrow sense of juridical law that specifies issues such as citizenship or business operations. Second, we refer to law in the broad political sense of control or order over a territory. This leads us to a second general conclusion, which is that entrepreneurship is only constituted through and by the legitimation of state. We have seen this with the illegal immigrant who is not deemed to be an entrepreneur simply because they are not legitimated by the state. This reminds us that it is hopelessly naïve to follow the neoliberal logic of thinking about enterprise and the state as opposites of one another. Rather, the state is constitutive of enterprise as was long ago argued by Polanyi (1945). If we follow this reasoning, we are reminded of the fact that the earliest 'adventurers' such as Francis Drake were indeed in the employment of the sovereign. Similarly, it is certainly no coincidence that we witnessed the first flourishing of entrepreneurship at the precise point in time of the rise of the modern nation state.

The fundamental interconnection between the state and entrepreneurship suggests further consequences. Any unique configuration of the state will tend to give rise to a unique configuration of entrepreneurship. The Italian city state will give rise to a different entrepreneur than the kind which we would find in Victorian England or contemporary North America. Moreover, each constitution of the state will give rise to different states of exception. It will render certain characters outside of the possibilities of entrepreneurship. In the Italian city-state we find that many of the entrepreneurs were actually Jewish financiers who existed in this state of exception. The mid-twentieth-century New York department-store owner was an entrepreneur while a jazz band leader was not. In today's global city, the freelance brand consultant is considered to be an entrepreneur while the immigrant selling counterfeit Gucci handbags on the street is not.

Our contemporary configuration of entrepreneurship seems even more strange when at the very moment that production appears to become increasingly global, socialised and immaterial, a point we will return to in the next two chapters. Today, there is an increasing recognition that we all create and trade in value – whether it be through caring for children, contributing to an open source community or working in an office. However, being an entrepreneur seems to be reserved only for the few with the right papers. Indeed, many enterprising souls on this planet find themselves in a permanent state of exception. This excludes them from the cultural status, economic rewards and political voice that come with the identity of being an entrepreneur.

This cuts to the heart of entrepreneurship discourse. Perhaps the most radical conclusion is that the central problem with enterprise discourse today is not that there are too many people who are designated as entrepreneurs (see, for example, du Gay, 1996). Rather, the issue is that there may not be enough who are able to claim to be entrepreneurial. Instead of seeing entrepreneurship discourse as being too general and too expansive, perhaps it is not general enough. Rectifying this situation would call for a generalisation of enterprise. However, were such a generalisation to happen, the question of what it means to be entrepreneurial would also be subject to a broad transformation. We might therefore concur with Daniel Hjorth (2003) when he suggests that the patron saint of entrepreneurs should cease to be Bill Gates and should instead become a lost soul like Don Quixote. The figure of the entrepreneur would then not be the legal inventor, but something quite other.

8. Enterprise of the other

We see in the cases of the Marquis de Sade and the illegal immigrant the way that entrepreneurship involves a whole range of moral assessments. One of the major reasons we recoil from designating someone such as Sade as an entrepreneur is that he is so obviously bad. The logic of taking up the example of Sade may now become more clear. Sade gets straight to the point when it comes to issues such as ethics. The case of Sade makes a short circuit which brings to the stage issues of morality and entrepreneurship. Our earlier discussions have stressed that entrepreneurs exist in a troubled relation to the dominant ethical schemes in a society. This assumption of ethical exceptionality has been used to tell us about everything from the entrepreneur's personality type to their position in social networks. But what such research rarely comes clean about are the ethics of entrepreneurship. That is, accounts of entrepreneurship only scratch the surface of the question of 'good' or 'bad' when it comes to entrepreneurship itself.

As we hope is now clear, far from being a morally neutral category, the entrepreneur is a figure who is riddled with ethical questions and injunctions. Ethics is in fact absolutely central to debates about the entrepreneur, even when not acknowledged as such. It is therefore vital that we clarify and examine the central normative criteria that are used to explicitly or implicitly assess entrepreneurship. By doing so, we are able to make clearer assessments about the ethics of the entrepreneur and entrepreneurship. We might then be in a position to consider the basis on which an ethical mode of enterprise might be constructed.

In this chapter, we propose to take some preliminary steps in this direction. Although existing studies examine the empirical causes and processes of entrepreneurship, they largely fail to clarify and justify the normative criteria with which we judge the entrepreneur. The few sustained normative theories of the entrepreneur rely on an assumption of individual rights and sovereignty. In this chapter, after discussing some of these normative accounts of entrepreneurship, we propose to turn things around by asking if the ethics of entrepreneurship starts not from the entrepreneur but from the *others* with which the entrepreneur inevitably interacts.

To do this we will draw on the ethical theory of Emmanuel Levinas, in particular his thinking of an 'ethics of the other'. Considering the entrepreneur as acting in relation to the other rather than in a purely self-interested way might provide a viable means of thinking the ethics of entrepreneurship. In particular, we argue that entrepreneurship should not be considered as the furthering of self-interest, often through abolishing the possible capacities of the other. It is perhaps quite surprising that Schumpeter's definition of entrepreneurship has resulted in such a privileging of one who does the combining of the factors of production rather than thinking seriously about the relation to the others who are going to get combined.

THE ENTREPRENEURIAL ETHIC

Today we are surrounded by talk of 'ethical businesses', 'social entrepreneurship', and 'fair enterprise'. Popular wisdom suggests that a blend of entrepreneurial pragmatism and social and ethical commitments could produce ethical businesses. There has also been resurgence in academic interest in the ethics of entrepreneurship, which has produced a growing body of research that considers questions such as why some entrepreneurs are 'ethical' and others are not, how entrepreneurs negotiate the ethical quandaries they find themselves in, and whether entrepreneurship may be considered ethical at all.

Perhaps the central concern in the growing field of entrepreneurial ethics has been why different entrepreneurs display such different ethical attitudes. This has led to a wide-ranging effort to identify the antecedents of entrepreneurial ethics. Historical explanations have sought to situate how an ethic of entrepreneurship arises during the expansion of capitalism in both Europe (Carr, 2003) and China (Cheung and King, 2004). National cultural context has also been shown to be a particularly salient factor (Bucar et al., 2003; Wu, 2002; Sommer and Welsh, 2000), with some unethical behaviours such as bribery being considered commonplace amongst entrepreneurs in certain states. The stage of the business cycle that the entrepreneur finds themselves in is also apparently important, with entrepreneurs less likely to engage in ethical behaviour earlier in the business cycle (Morris et al., 2002). Others have pointed out that the characteristics of the business environment shape the kinds of behaviour which are considered ethically acceptable. For instance, a dynamic or highly competitive business environment encourages unethical behaviour (Chau and Siu, 2000). Dishonesty is encouraged in environments where businesses must struggle to gain resources and legitimacy. Another factor that has been shown to shape the ethical stance of entrepreneurs is their personality traits (Solymossy and Masters, 2002; Yurtsever, 2003). Entrepreneurs are said to have a tendency towards egoism which increases the likelihood that they will engage in unethical behaviour (Longenecker et al., 1988, 1989a,

1989b). Alongside these personality differences, researchers have located the differences in entrepreneur's cognitive processes and reasoning abilities (Teal and Carroll, 1999), such as the entrepreneurs' strong belief in their own business ideas leading to self-serving biases, counterfactual thinking and self-justification (Baron, 1998). While each of these studies differs significantly in terms of the factors identified which lead to unethical behaviour, they are based on a common attempt to tease out the factors that cause unethical behaviour.

A second body of research on entrepreneurial ethics does not seek to identify the causes of unethical behaviour amongst entrepreneurs, but undertakes the more interpretive task of examining the process through which entrepreneurs actually negotiate ethical tensions. An excellent example of the difficult process of negotiating various ethical demands can be found in a study of Chinese Confucian entrepreneurs (Cheung and King, 2004). This study shows how these entrepreneurs struggle to reconcile and balance injunctions of maximising profit and their Confucian ethics. Other studies have examined the rather instrumental way entrepreneurs seek to build relations, acquire resources and sustain their new ventures (Starr and MacMillan, 1990). Finally research on entrepreneurship in transitional economies has identified the difficult and ongoing negotiation that entrepreneurs have to undergo around whether they will engage in unethical behaviour (Radaev, 1993). This research demonstrates that in transitional economies such as the former Soviet Union, the norms around what is considered ethical and unethical are constantly in flux and up for questioning.

A final body of thought has turned away from empirical considerations of the antecedents of unethical behaviour and the processes of negotiating ethical dilemmas. Instead, this literature offers a normative assessment of entrepreneurship. By doing so, it seeks to treat entrepreneurship as an ethical principle that must be subjected to proper analysis. Instead of drawing on psychological or sociological studies to explain why particular entrepreneurs are ethical or not, this approach tends to draw on normative political theory to assess the ethics of enterprise as a whole. One of the few substantive normative studies is Brenkert's (2002) broadly liberal analysis of the hidden ethical tensions at the heart of entrepreneurship. He argues that three central ethics associated with entrepreneurship are decentralisation, the extension of the economy and the intensification of the economy. Closely examining each of these internal ethics, he identifies potential shortcomings that would make such demands unsustainable. The demand for decentralisation leads to a declining role of government, which leads to massive inequities in wealth which cannot be ethically justified. The demand for the extension of the economy results in the privatisation of large sectors of social life resulting in the decline of rules and institutions which support the economy. The demand for intensification of the economy results in the speeding up of life and dominance of the entrepreneurial class over all others in society. Following from his liberal political philosophy, Brenkert suggests the need to balance a demand for enterprise with the necessity for rational rule-bound institutions. The ultimate message here seems to be that enterprise and the entrepreneurial society is not sufficient on its own, but must be supplemented with appropriate legislative checks and balances in order to avoid the excesses of a pure entrepreneurial society.

A contrasting argument is provided by Velamuri, who draws on libertarian political philosophy in an attempt to reconcile enterprise and altruism. He argues that instead of setting up altruism and entrepreneurialism as opposites, we should recognise that enterprise at its heart is about creating value for other people. Entrepreneurship is defined as the individual 'exercise of freedom with the view to creating value' (Velamuri, 2002: 128). Value which is created is only value because it is shared. It is through an entrepreneur's exchange with the 'fellow citizen' (2002: 131) that value is validated and created. The implication which Velamuri draws is the familiar insight found in libertarian social thought that by pursuing selfish interests, the entrepreneur contributes to the whole of society, and therefore can be judged as altruistic. Any attempt to limit the freedom of enterprise would be judged as an affront to individual liberty as well as collective well-being and therefore should be resisted as zealously as infringements upon free speech.

While Brenkert (2002) and Velamuri's (2002) assessments of entrepreneurship differ substantially in their conclusions, they certainly employ a similar method of using normative political philosophy to assess entrepreneurship. Unlike other studies of entrepreneurial ethics that tend to opt for empirical description and explanation of the ethics of particular entrepreneurs, a normative stance allows us to begin exploring the broader question of justification, which has been recognised as central to social life (Boltanski and Thévenot, 2006). Normative political philosophy allows us to begin to ask on what basis entrepreneurship might reasonably be justified as being ethical, and what indeed would an ethical enterprise look like. However, Brenkert and Velamuri only provide a very limited normative assessment of the entrepreneur. What holds these two approaches together is the emphasis on the rights of the entrepreneur as a sovereign and free producer. Some, such as Velamuri, vigorously justify and defend this individual freedom. Others, such as Brenkert seek to argue that this individual freedom needs certain institutional constraints to thrive. But what this discussion of the extent to which the individual rights of the entrepreneur should be extended or limited completely passes over is what Levinas (1999) calls the 'rights of the other person'. What is not usually considered in discussions of the entrepreneurial ethic is how entrepreneurship might not be so much about the more or less free exercise of individual freedom as how the entrepreneur is always engaged in acting with and on others. What if ethical entrepreneurship does not involve freedom of the self, but rather a forever expanding responsibility for and freedom of the other?

ENTREPRENEURSHIP OF THE OTHER

For Levinas ethics is 'first philosophy' (Levinas, 1989), coming before being and before knowledge of being. But Levinas is concerned to recover something in the meaning of ethics, by going back to the basic recognition that ethics is grounded in the relation between a subject and an other person. For Levinas, ethics necessarily involves a relation to the other in which the other is not mere matter for my manipulation. The encounter with the other as other is also not a matter of smooth assimilation, which would be to reduce the other to the same. Ethics is a rather more disquieting relation with the other in which the subject who responds has their very sense of self called into question.

This is not the place to go in great detail into Levinas (but for engagements see Aasland, 2009; *Business Ethics: A European Review*, 2007; Jones, 2003). What is most important for our purposes here is the effort that Levinas makes to show how ethics involves a decentring of the subject. Ethics, following Levinas, involves a decentring of the location of the ethical from the individual subject. Ethics has often been seen as a matter of what I should do, how I should act. But if ethics is genuinely a matter of the other, then ethics does not start from me, but from the other. As Levinas once put it, his ethics is not opposed to humanism, human rights, the rights of the individual and the strength of the subject. The shift he seeks to introduce, however, is to shift this humanism, and give it to the other person. Hence, in an important twist, Levinas argues for a humanism, but importantly a humanism of the other person (Levinas, 2006, also 1999).

Levinasian ethics obviously has much to say when engaging a matter such as entrepreneurship. We propose here to focus in particular on Levinas's dislocation of ethics. We should emphasise that although Levinas makes an ethical argument, and always returns to ethics as first philosophy, the way in which Levinas does this always involves at least a small risk to the object of inquiry, which can be reframed in significant ways and taken outside itself, beyond itself, towards the other. The

Levinasian displacement would be from entrepreneurship towards the 'entrepreneurship of the other'. This is not to denigrate or to partialise the entrepreneurship of those called entrepreneurs. Rather, when we introduce ethics into the picture we begin to shift focus in order to recognise the entrepreneurship of others.

Throughout the book, and in particular in the last two chapters, we discussed cases of those excluded from being designated entrepreneurs. We use these examples to make an argument against those such as du Gay who see contemporary cultural economy marked by a generalisation of entrepreneurship following a set of efforts to 'enterprise up society'. We have been concerned to show that the generalisation of entrepreneurship involves a set of quite specific exclusions, insofar as particular types of character, and particular types of social innovation, are effectively excluded from the otherwise praised entrepreneurialisation of society. With the generalisation of entrepreneurship comes restriction, a restriction that has no grounds and has the potential to 'bite back' those who would celebrate the universal goodness of entrepreneurship.

Given the exclusions of entrepreneurship discourse, and given the direction we have been led by Levinas in recognising the entrepreneurship of the other, would the most radical unmasking of entrepreneurship therefore be not the opposition to entrepreneurship discourse but rather, its embrace? If we were to move in this direction, we might move towards a conception of what we propose to call 'general entrepreneurship'. When we do so we are drawing on the distinction that Bataille makes between restrictive and general economy, and which we discussed in Chapter 5. We propose a similar distinction between restrictive and general conceptions of entrepreneurship. In such an expanded or general conception of entrepreneurship, where would creativity lie?

GENERAL ENTREPRENEURSHIP

General entrepreneurship would break with the restrictions of the characters and activities that might be legitimately seen as entrepreneurship. It would see the creative capacity in *all* labour, regardless of location, actor or end. It would see innovations across the social sphere writ large, rather than in the small localised spheres in which it is typically seen. It would start from the innovation of the other person.

We are therefore led here to what Marx called the 'general intellect' (see Marx, 1973: 693), a phrase that has become particularly important in contemporary critical accounts of the post-Fordist transformations of work and economy (see for example Hardt and Negri, 1994; 2000; Negri,

2008; Virno, 2008). This much misunderstood phrase refers to the capacities for productivity and creativity of what Marx calls living labour. Marx speaks of labour as 'the living, form-giving fire' (1973: 361) that is the source of creativity. Following in particular the writings of Antonio Negri, living labour is grounded in a basic human affirmation of possibility and creativity (see for example Negri, 2004).

Let us not think, however, as pundits of the post-industrial society and some of Negri's followers have, that the general intellect is simply a matter of ideas or the creativity of a particular class of knowledge workers (cf. Florida, 2004). The general intellect is a result of the 'mass intellectuality' that results from the socialisation of production throughout the twentieth century (Mandarini, 2005). Here cooperation extends beyond the factory gates, as intellectuality and productivity through science, technology, and so forth spreads across the 'social factory' (Hardt and Negri, 1994). With cooperation on an ever-extending scale, we here also find that the idea of entrepreneurship becomes increasingly implausible. Entrepreneurship becomes less and less an activity of the individual, and more a matter of innovation with, of and by the other.

The problem that remains is that entrepreneurship discourse paradoxically seems brutally resistant to allow such a generalisation. This is because, as we have been trying to stress, entrepreneurship discourse *must* restrict, it must exclude. Entrepreneurship is a matter of control and capture, of localisation and restriction of innovation. This is perhaps just another way of expressing the common complaint about the individualism of entrepreneurship discourse. Talk of the individual entrepreneurship is a condensation of a general creativity onto the individual. It is a matter of locating in one individual what is in fact the results of the activity of many.

According to the restrictive definition of the entrepreneur, the entrepreneur is the one who is able to capture the innovation of the other. This attempt to capture the innovation of the other can be seen in so many practices of entrepreneurship, perhaps the most obvious of which are in the restriction of further innovation through the various practices associated with patent and other laws that restrict or otherwise seize control of the means of innovation. Likewise, merger and acquisition, which are the staple fare of many entrepreneurs, involve an effort to fulfil the perfect destiny of the market, that is, to create a monopoly so as to destroy the capacity of the other to create something new.

Against this restrictive conception of entrepreneurship, we might pose an alternative definition, that is, of the general entrepreneur. The general entrepreneur is the one who creates the capacity for the other to innovate. Generalised entrepreneurship involves an innovation in which the innovation is not one's own but one that makes possible the innovation of the other. Such entrepreneurship generalises itself beyond any individual or particular set of practices.

Which of these conceptions of entrepreneurship – restrictive and general – do we want? We argue that this question is strictly undecidable. When we say that it is undecidable we are thinking of the way that Derrida conceives of undecidability as 'a determinate oscillation between possibilities' (Derrida, 1988: 274). The tension of undecidability is, for Derrida, the very grounds of anything called ethics. That is to say, ethics finds its place not in the reassuring grounds of, for example, blanket celebration or dismissal of entrepreneurship, nor in resolution of ambivalence through negotiation of conflicts or balancing of demands. Ethics emerges in the space in which one does not know which way to go, which other to respond to.

Here, then, we propose to conceive of the ethics of entrepreneurship as this moment of tension between the restrictive and general entrepreneurship. This is in part because of the way that the restrictive conception of entrepreneurship always already involves the appeal to the general. This will perhaps unmask the seductive kernel of the idea of entrepreneurship. Entrepreneurship promises social innovation and improvement. It promises to create a space in which we all might innovate and in which the other would be permitted to participate in discourse over what improvement or innovation might mean. Insofar as entrepreneurship remains restrictive and denies or captures the innovation of the other, it falls well short of being worthy of the name of entrepreneurship.

9. What remains

We have found that entrepreneurship is an empty concept, but at the same time one that is filled with economic, political, legal and moral ramifications. Throughout this book we have sought to critically examine the category of the entrepreneur. As we have proceeded, we have sought to unmask the entrepreneur so as to show the limits of entrepreneurship discourse, both in the popular and academic spheres. But after all these unmaskings, in this final chapter we might ask what remains of the entrepreneur? Talk of entrepreneurship, both in the business world and in academic ruminations, promises a great deal. This is perhaps because of the religious grounds of the promise to create all things anew (Sørensen, 2008, see also Bill, 2006). With entrepreneurship comes the promise of a new life for the individual entrepreneur, and often new or improved social relations for those that will benefit from entrepreneurship. We find again and again the promise offered up of individual autonomy, of self-valuation and of an escape from a currently humdrum and boring life.

It is important to understand this response. In fact it is quite an understandable response to the situation that many of us live in today. There is often a sense of being trapped in excessively rule-bound and over-bureaucratised societies, and a sense that things could certainly be different, and quite possibly better.

But how do we respond to this sentiment? The temptation, too often, is only to see responses that are individualised. That is to say, the solution to our collective problems is taken to fall on the shoulders of an individual, the entrepreneur. This is often still the case when we talk about social entrepreneurship, which is about innovation in the social sphere, but in which the innovation is once again set in motion not by a collective but typically by an individual, or at best a pair, such as Ben and Jerry.

This is paradoxical and, we argue, crippling for entrepreneurship. This is because first of all entrepreneurship without the other is unthinkable. Enterprise is a fundamentally collective enterprise, based on social cooperation, and in this sense the image of the entrepreneur making lemonade by themselves and selling it at the front gate is a fundamentally misleading myth. Not only will such an entrepreneur have to start employing other workers if that enterprise is to achieve any significant scale, but moreover, the act of making and selling even that most basic lemonade requires a vast array of social cooperative relations to be in place before it would be even thinkable.

SOCIALISATION OF ENTREPRENEURSHIP

As we noted in the previous chapter, one of the things that many observers of social and economic changes over the twentieth century have noted is the progressively increasing *socialisation* of work and of economic life more generally. This is clearly what is at stake when we talk about interconnectedness and globalisation. But even before that talk there was cooperation on a vast scale in systems of mass production, and we saw increasingly collective efforts in production in the workplace. At the same time, outside the workplace, the twentieth century also witnessed major transformations in sociality, with increasing connections with others from a range of backgrounds, and with the establishment of forms of shared sociality through radio, television and other media that made social relations almost impossible to avoid.

With this progressive socialisation of economic and social life, continuing belief and faith in the individual is truly remarkable. And insofar as the entrepreneur is a category that is about individual impulse and action, it is a figure that is more suited for the abstraction of a Robinson Crusoe on an island rather than for the socialised economy we live in in the twenty-first century. If the ideology of entrepreneurship is, at the most basic, the idea of the self-made man, the one who fights against all the odds, then this idea is out of touch with the realities of cooperative labour today. It is instead motivated by something else, a preference to reward a small number rather than the actually productive force that we now have on our doorstep. It is for this reason that entrepreneurship, both in popular forms and also in the most apparently scientific statistical varieties, remains profoundly ideological.

In this book we have made an effort to call into question these presuppositions about the entrepreneur. In Chapter 3 we sought to show how elusive the figure of the entrepreneur is, and discuss the strange persistence in talking about entrepreneurship despite the fact that it is incredibly unclear what it is that is being talked about. In Chapters 4 and 5 we showed the implication of the category of the entrepreneur in struggles over social and economic valuation and reward, which set the entrepreneur within broader patterns of contestation over who deserves to be rewarded for the vastly increased productivity that capitalism has witnessed throughout the twentieth century. In Chapters 6 and 7 we turned to two cases of 'unlikely entrepreneurs' in order to dig deeper into the political and moral presuppositions of entrepreneurship discourse. Drawing all of these motifs together, in Chapter 8 we took up the question of the other in order to both put to bed the myth of the entrepreneur as the centre of action and to show ways in which we can think beyond the entrepreneur as the focus of attention.

These unmaskings were not intended for their own sake, but because it is pressingly important today to think and act differently with respect to entrepreneurship. In order to speak as clearly as we can, to both simplify and to call for action, we will conclude our book in the way that the most simple report would, with a consideration of the implications of our analysis for research, policy and entrepreneurs.

IMPLICATIONS FOR RESEARCH

Our argument throughout has been that the object of entrepreneurship is not where it is usually thought to be. This is why we spoke of the entrepreneur as an alluring and 'sublime object', and why we set out on a series of 'unmaskings'. The idea that entrepreneurship is a stable and fixed object that could be simply studied is misguided. Entrepreneurship researchers need to be far more attuned to the complexity of social analysis. This involves going beyond interpretation, and the call to be practical cannot be used as an alibi for avoiding reflection and for simplification and dogmatism.

Our second implication is that entrepreneurship research could be a great deal more creative and inventive than it has been. We noted in our introduction that entrepreneurship research is remarkably bureaucratic and unoriginal. Entrepreneurship research could, as some have been arguing in recent years, be something far more, well, 'entrepreneurial'. This would require a change in mindset, one that found merit in inventiveness and in new and different ways of thinking. And with this, we would need to think not of the usual entrepreneurial situations and cases, but be open to the wide world of the strange and unusual. In this direction, Alf Rehn has made an important contribution by emphasising the need to study the world in all its insanity, rather than follow the stylised patterns of what is thought to be 'real entrepreneurship' (see for example, Rehn, 2004, 2008).

Third, entrepreneurship is infinitely more socialised than is typically recognised in entrepreneurship research. We need to go far beyond studies of social enterprise. We need studies that recognise the social imbeddedness of entrepreneurship, and the social relations that produce and maintain entrepreneurship, right down to the very idea of entrepreneurship. We need to recognise the role of popular culture and entertainment in which circulates persistent images of James Bond type figures who are able to achieve massive success against all odds, not forgetting the policy initiatives and laws that reinforce and reward individual entrepreneurs.

The fourth implication is that entrepreneurship research is far more socialised than is typically recognised. It is often mistakenly thought that entrepreneurship researchers are somehow able to escape their institutional and cultural positions in order to study entrepreneurship as it is. Over the past ten years as we have worked on this book we have been continually astonished at not only the closed nature of entrepreneurship research but also the way in which the norms of the academic community of entrepreneurship researchers have been treated as self-evident. So not only do we need a critique of popular conceptions of entrepreneurship, but the norms of the entrepreneurship academy also need to be understood, and where they are found wanting, they need to be unsettled.

With this, it is important that our critique is not simply invented from thin air, and equally, that in the effort to be creative, we do not licence ourselves to say just anything. Thus, our fifth implication for research is that entrepreneurship research is desperately in need of serious engagement with the traditions of critical social theory and philosophy. In this book we have tried to show how that might work, even if there is clearly much more that needs to be done, but that goes beyond our limited efforts here. Rethinking the entrepreneur is not the result of the thinking of one or a pair of minds, but requires a difficult collective labour.

IMPLICATIONS FOR POLICY

We hardly need mention the extent to which the idea of enterprise has infused the public sector over the past thirty years. From the critical analysis that we have provided here, and also from the now-apparent empirical evidence of the difficulties that have resulted from introducing enterprise in the public sector, it should be clear that there are serious limitations to introducing 'enterprise' and 'entrepreneurship' into that sector. The fact that this is not widely accepted, and that governments continue to have faith in enterprise – often in blatant disregard for anything that would count as evidence – should remind us of the continuing need for public sector employees and those who have a stake in public institutions (that is to say, all of us) now to confidently oppose the discourse of entrepreneurship. This involves comprehending what talk of entrepreneurship means, understanding the limits of entrepreneurship, and knowing when talk of entrepreneurship is simply meaningless.

Second, those responsible for public policy need to recognise the radically social nature of entrepreneurship. From this a number of consequences arise. Some of these relate to promoting innovation and creativity, better ways of designing and producing the necessities of life. If such innovations are to be produced they will be produced *socially*, and importantly will come out of research, research that is often expensive. If that research is to have a social benefit, then the interests to which research is put must be subject to deliberation in advance.

A third policy implication, which springs from the second, is that policy has an important place in allocating the rewards for production and innovations in production. In Chapter 4 we documented some of the history of contestation over the claims to value, and today we are again and again told that particular individuals, because they are rewarded enormously by the market, are of enormous value. If we recall the social nature of enterprise, then we recognise that the market is not a particularly good measure of individual activity, when we see the callous disregard with which many currently powerful entrepreneurs treat their fellow human beings. One thing that public policy and legislation is for is curtailing these excesses, and for socialising, which involves distributing, the rewards of socialised production. Clearly, today, this requires both national and international interventions.

IMPLICATIONS FOR ENTREPRENEURS

Throughout this book we have clearly been quite critical of the idea of entrepreneurship. We should conclude by stressing that when we criticise entrepreneurship we are criticising the category and discourse, and not individual entrepreneurs. If there is one take-home message for entrepreneurs here, then it is the importance of avoiding the easy embrace of ideology. There are clearly reasons, to do with privilege and wealth, for which one might embrace the promise of entrepreneurship. But we hope that we have also shown that there are important reasons for not embracing the figure of the entrepreneur in the way that it normally appears. This is not just because to criticise ideas and oneself is an important part of making oneself more free, but also because entrepreneurs are implicated with others, and with governing the prospects for their freedom.

The second implication is that entrepreneurship is not about entrepreneurs. It is about relations with others, as we have sought to show throughout, and in particular in Chapter 8. At least since the massive socialisation of work throughout the twentieth century, entrepreneurs today need others more than ever before. The issue is that those others, and perhaps even more than ever today, are often inclined to think that they, on the other hand, do not need the entrepreneurs. They therefore question the property laws that protect innovations, and the economic inequalities that entrepreneurs often perpetuate by appealing to the laws of the market. If there has historically been a 'reserve army' of labour willing to carry out the will of the entrepreneurial leader, this would seriously be in jeopardy if a pattern of global democratisation were to become much more pronounced.

If you are an entrepreneur, then, perhaps this book might have helped you to think about the vast array of things outside of you, and outside of enterprise, that have made you and your enterprise possible. This then is our third and final implication: entrepreneurs live in this world, not in the fantasy world of Robinson Crusoe or the fairy tale of the lemonade stand. And in this world we are with others, right from the beginning. And it is only a cruel and vindictive actor who can survey the landscape, from however tall an office or however elegant a jet, and disregard the others who made that building and that jet, and not feel a responsibility to listen and to hear them. Perhaps, then, what we find when we unmask the entrepreneur is the face of the other.

References

Aasland, D. (2009) *Ethics and Economy After Levinas*. London: MayFlyBooks.

Abercrombie, N., S. Hill and B. Turner (1980) *The Dominant Ideology Thesis*. London: Allen and Unwin.

Abrams, F. (2002) *Below the Breadline: Living on the Minimum Wage*. London: Profile.

Ackroyd, S. and S. Fleetwood (eds) (2000) *Realist Perspectives on Management and Organisations*. London: Routledge.

Adis, R. and M. van Praag (2007) 'Illegal entrepreneurship experience: Does it make a difference for business performance and motivation?', *Journal of Business Venturing*, 22: 283–310.

Adorno, T.W. and M. Horkheimer (1972) *Dialectic of Enlightenment*, trans. J. Cummings. New York: Continuum.

Agamben, G. (1998) *Homo Sacer: Sovereign Power and Bare Life*, trans. D. Heller-Roazen. Stanford, CA: Stanford University Press.

Agamben, G. (2000) *Means Without End: Notes on Politics*, trans. V. Binetti and C. Casarino. Minneapolis: University of Minnesota Press.

Agamben, G. (2005) *State of Exception*, trans. K. Atell. Chicago: University of Chicago Press.

Aldrich, H. (2005) 'Entrepreneurship' in N.J. Smelser and R. Swedberg (eds.), *Handbook of Economic Sociology* (second edition). Princeton, NJ: Princeton University Press.

Althusser, L. (1971) 'Ideology and ideological state apparatuses (notes towards an investigation)' in *Lenin and Philosophy and Other Essays*, trans. B. Brewster. London: Monthly Review.

Alvesson, M., T. Bridgman and H. Willmott (eds) (2009) *The Oxford Handbook of Critical Management Studies*. Oxford: Oxford University Press.

Andrew, E. (1995) *The Genealogy of Values: The Aesthetic Economy of Nietzsche and Proust*. Lanham, MD: Rowman and Littlefield.

Armstrong, P. (2001) 'Styles of illusion', *Sociological Review*, 49(2): 155–73.

Armstrong, P. (2005) *Critique of Entrepreneurship: People and Policy*. London: Palgrave-Macmillan.

Arnaud, G. (2002) 'The organization and the symbolic: Organizational dynamics viewed from a Lacanian perspective', *Human Relations*, 55(6): 691–716.

Austin, J., H. Stevenson and J. Wei-Skillern (2006) 'Social and commercial entrepreneurship: Same, different, or both?', *Entrepreneurship Theory and Practice*, 30(1): 1–22.

Badham, R., K. Garrety, V. Morrigan, M. Zanko and P. Dawson (2003) 'Designer deviance: Enterprise and deviance in culture change programmes', *Organization*, 10(4): 707–30.

Baran, P. and P. Sweezy (1966) *Monopoly Capital.* New York: Modern Reader.

Baron, R.A. (1998) 'Cognitive mechanisms in entrepreneurship: Why and when entrepreneurs think differently than other people', *Journal of Business Venturing*, 13: 275–94.

Bataille, G. (1985) 'The notion of expenditure' in *Visions of Excess: Selected Writings 1927–1939,* Minneapolis, MN: University of Minnesota Press.

Bataille, G. (1989) *The Accursed Share: An Essay on General Economy, Volume 1: Consumption*, trans. R. Hurley. New York: Zone Books.

Bataille, G. (1991) *The Accursed Share: An Essay on General Economy, Volume 2: The History of Eroticism, and Volume 3: Sovereignty* trans. R. Hurley. New York: Zone Books.

Bataille, G. (2001) *Eroticism*, trans. M. Dalwood. London: Penguin.

BBC News (2001) 'Profile: Tito the spaceman', 28 April. Online. Available at: http://www.bbc.co.uk.

Bendix, R. (1956) *Work and Authority in Industry: Ideologies of Management in the Course of Industrialization.* New York: Wiley.

Benjamin, W. (2002) *The Arcades Project*, trans. H. Eiland and K. McLaughlin. Cambridge, MA: Belknap Harvard.

Benson, J.K. (1977) 'Organizations: A dialectical view', *Administrative Science Quarterly*, 22(1): 1–21.

Berlin, I. (1969) *Four Essays on Liberty.* Oxford: Oxford University Press.

Bill, F. (2006), *The Apocalypse of Entrepreneurship.* Växjö: Växjö University Press.

Blanchot, Maurice (1967) 'The main impropriety (excerpts)', trans. J. Guicharnaud, *Yale French Studies*, 39: 50–63.

Boltanski, L. and L. Thévenot (2006) *On Justification: Economies of Worth*, trans. C. Porter. Princeton, NJ: Princeton University Press.

Bouchikhi, H. (1993) 'A constructivist framework for understanding entrepreneurship performance', *Organization Studies*, 14(4): 549–70.

Bourdieu, P. (1990) *In Other Words: Essays Towards a Reflexive Sociology*, trans. M. Adamson. Stanford, CA: Stanford University Press.

Branson, R. (2007) *Screw It, Let's Do It, Expanded: Lessons in Life and Business*. London: Virgin.

Brazeal, D.V. and T.T. Herbert (1999) 'The genesis of entrepreneurship', *Entrepreneurship Theory and Practice*, 23(3): 29–46.

Brenkert, G. (2002) 'Entrepreneurship, ethics and the good society', *Ruffin Series in Business Ethics*, 4, 5–43.

Brennan, T. (1993) *History After Lacan*. London: Routledge.

Brewis, J. and S. Linstead (2000) *Sex, Work and Sex Work: Eroticising Organization*. London: Routledge.

Brockhaus, R.H. and P.S. Horwitz (1986) 'The psychology of the entrepreneur' in D.L. Sexton and R.W. Smilor (eds), *The Art and Science of Entrepreneurship*. Cambridge, MA: Ballinger.

Brown, M. (1998) *Richard Branson*. London: Headline.

Bucar, B., M. Glas and R.D. Hisrich (2003) 'Ethics and entrepreneurs: An international comparative study', *Journal of Business Venturing*, 18: 261–81.

Bunyan, N. (2005) 'Cocklers' desperate struggle to escape rising tide', *Daily Telegraph*, 21 September, p. 13.

Bunyan, N. (2006) 'Phone calls of farewell as the tide closed in', *Daily Telegraph*, 25 March, p. 4.

Burchell, G. (1993) 'Liberal government and techniques of the self', *Economy and Society*, 22(3): 267–82.

Burrell, Gibson (1997) *Pandemonium: Towards a Retro-Organization Theory*. London: Sage.

Business Ethics: A European Review (2007) Special issue: Levinas, business, ethics, 16(3).

Bygrave, W. (1989a) 'The entrepreneurship paradigm (I): A philosophical look at its research methodologies', *Entrepreneurship Theory and Practice*, 14(1): 7–26.

Bygrave, W. (1989b) 'The entrepreneurship paradigm (II): Chaos and catastrophes among quantum leaps', *Entrepreneurship Theory and Practice*, 14(2): 7–30.

Bygrave, W. and M. Minniti (2000) 'The social dynamics of entrepreneurship', *Entrepreneurship Theory and Practice*, 24(3): 25–36.

Campbell, John (2004) *Institutional Change and Globalization*. Princeton, NJ: Princeton University Press.

Cantillon, Richard (1755/1952) *Essai sur la nature du commerce en général*. Paris: Institut National d'études Démographiques.

Carr, A. and L. Zanetti. (1999) 'Metatheorizing the dialectic of self and other: The psychodynamics in work organizations', *American Behavioral Scientist*, 43(2): 324–45.

Carr, P. (2003) 'Revisiting the protestant ethic and the spirit of capitalism:

Understanding the relationship between ethics and enterprise', *Journal of Business Ethics*, 47(1): 7–16.

CBS News (2001) 'Interview with Dennis Tito', 28 April. Online. Available at: http://www.cbsnews.com.

Cederström, C. and R. Grassman (2007) 'The masochistic reflexive turn', *ephemera: theory and politics in organization*, 8(1): 41–57.

Cederström, C. and C. Hoedemaekers (eds) (forthcoming) *Lacan and Organization*. London: MayFlyBooks.

Chandler, A. (1977) *The Visible Hand: The Managerial Revolution in American Business*. Cambridge: MA: Belknap.

Chapman, J. and J. Tozer (2004) 'The warning they ignored', *Daily Mail*, 12 February, p. 4.

Chau, L.L. and W. Siu. (2000) 'Ethical decision making in corporate entrepreneurial organizations', *Journal of Business Ethics,* 23: 365–75.

Cheung, T.S. and A.Y.-C. King (2004) 'Righteousness and profitableness: The moral choices of contemporary Confucian entrepreneurs', *Journal of Business Ethics*, 54(3): 245–60.

Cohen, L. and G. Musson (2002) 'Entrepreneurial identities: Reflections from two case studies', *Organization*, 7(1): 31–48.

Cole, A.H. (1969) 'Definition of entrepreneurship' in J. Komives (ed.), *Karl A. Bostrom Seminar in the Study of Enterprise*. Milwaukee, WI: Centre for Venture Management.

Contu, A. (2008) 'Decaf resistance: On misbehavior, cynicism and desire in liberal workplaces', *Management Communication Quarterly*, 21(3): 364–79.

Copjec, J. (1994) *Read My Desire: Lacan Against the Historicists*. Cambridge, MA: MIT Press.

Craven, N. and J. Tozer (2006) 'Deadly greed of the gangmaster', *Daily Mail*, 25 March, p. 4.

Cusset, C. (1998) 'Editor's preface: The lesson of libertinage', *Yale French Studies*, 94: 1–14.

de Beauvoir, S. (1966) 'Must we burn Sade?' in Marquis de Sade (ed. and trans. A. Wainhouse and R. Seaver), *The 120 Days of Sodom*. New York: Grove.

Deleuze, G. (1991) 'Coldness and cruelty' in *Masochism*. New York: Zone Books.

Deleuze, G. and F. Guattari (1983) *Anti-Oedipus: Capitalism and Schizophrenia, Vol. 1*, trans. R. Hurley, M. Seem and H. Lane. Minneapolis: University of Minnesota Press.

Deleuze, G. and F. Guattari (1986) *Kafka: Toward a Minor Literature*, trans. D. Polan. Minneapolis: University of Minnesota Press.

Deleuze, G. and F. Guattari (1988) *A Thousand Plateaus: Capitalism and*

Schizophrenia, Vol. 2, trans. B. Massumi. Minneapolis: University of Minnesota Press.

Deleuze, G. and F. Guattari (1994) *What is Philosophy?*, trans. G. Burchell and H. Tomlinson. London: Verso.

Derrida, J. (1981) *Positions*, trans. A. Bass. Chicago: University of Chicago Press.

Derrida, J. (1988) *Limited Inc.*, trans. E. Weber. Evanston, IL: Northwestern University Press.

Derrida, J. (1992a) 'Force of law: the "mystical foundation of authority"', trans. M. Quaintance, in D. Cornell, M. Rosenfeld and D.G. Carlson (eds), *Deconstruction and the Possibility of Justice*. New York: Routledge.

Derrida, J. (1992b) *Given Time: 1. Counterfeit Money*, trans. P. Kamuf. Chicago: University of Chicago Press.

Derrida, J. (1995) *The Gift of Death*, trans. D. Wills. Chicago: University of Chicago Press.

Diprose, R. (2002) *Corporeal Generosity: On Giving with Nietzsche, Merleau-Ponty and Levinas*. New York: State University of New York Press.

Doolin, B. (2002) 'Enterprise discourse, professional identity and the organizational control of hospital clinicians', *Organization Studies*, 23(3): 369–90.

Dorado, S. (2005) 'Institutional entrepreneurship, partaking and convening', *Organization Studies*, 26(3): 385–414.

Down, S. (2006) *Narratives of Enterprise: Crafting Entrepreneurial Self-Identity in a Small Firm*. Cheltenham, UK and Northampton, MA, USA: Edward Elgar.

Downing, S. (2005) 'The social construction of entrepreneurship: Narrative and dramatic processes in the coproduction of organizations and identities', *Entrepreneurship Theory and Practice*, 29(2): 185–204.

Driver, M. (2008) 'New and useless: A psychoanalytic perspective on organizational creativity', *Journal of Management Inquiry*, 17(3): 187–97.

du Gay, P. (1991) 'Enterprise culture and the ideology of excellence', *New Formations*, 13: 45–61.

du Gay, P. (1994) 'Making up managers: Bureaucracy, enterprise and the liberal art of separation', *British Journal of Sociology*, 45(4): 655–74.

du Gay, P. (1996) *Consumption and Identity at Work*. London: Sage.

du Gay, P. (2000a) 'Enterprise and its futures: A response to Fournier and Grey', *Organization*, 7(1): 165–83.

du Gay, P. (2000b) *In Praise of Bureaucracy: Weber, Organization, Ethics*. London: Sage.

du Gay, P. (2003) 'The Tyranny of the Epochal: Change, Epochalism and Organizational Reform', *Organization*, 10(4): 663–84.

du Gay, P. (2004) 'Against "Enterprise" (but not against "enterprise", for that would make no sense)', *Organization*, 11(1): 37–57.

du Gay, P. and G. Salaman (1992) 'The Cult(ure) of the Customer', *Journal of Management Studies*, 29(5): 615–33.

du Gay, P., G. Salaman and B. Rees (1996) 'The conduct of management and the management of conduct: Contemporary managerial discourse and the constitution of the "competent" manager', *Journal of Management Studies*, 33(3): 263–82.

Duchesneau, D.A and W.B. Gartner (1990) 'A profile of new venture success and failure in emerging industries', *Journal of Business Venturing*, 5: 297–321.

Durier, M. (1999) *Sidewalk*. New York: Farrar, Straus and Giroux.

Eagleton, T. (1991) *Ideology: An Introduction*. London: Verso.

Economist (2004) 'Britian's Illegal Workers', 12 February.

Ehrenreich, B. (2002) *Nickel and Dimed: Undercover in Low-Wage USA*. London: Granta.

Eisenstadt, S.N. (1964) 'Institutionalization and change', *American Sociological Review*, 29(2): 235–47.

Eisenstadt, S.N., and L. Roninger (1981) 'Clientelism in communist systems: A comparative perspective', *Studies in Comparative Communism*, 21(3): 233–45.

Entrialgo, M., E. Fernandez and C.J. Vazquez (2001) 'The effect of the organizational context on SME's entrepreneurship: Some Spanish evidence', *Small Business Economics*, 16(3): 223–36.

Fadahunsi, A. and P. Rosa (2002) 'Entrepreneurship and illegality: Insights from the Nigerian cross-border trade', *Journal of Business Venturing*, 17: 397–429.

Fairclough, N. (1995). *Critical Discourse Analysis: The Critical Study of Language*. London: Longman.

Feher, Michel (ed.) (1997) *The Libertine Reader: Eroticism and Enlightenment in Eighteenth-Century France*. New York: Zone Books.

Ferguson, P.P. (1998) 'A cultural field in the making: Gastronomy in 19th-century France', *American Journal of Sociology*, 104: 597–641.

Fleming, P. and A. Spicer (2003) 'Working at a cynical distance: Implications for power, resistance and subjectivity', *Organization*, 10(1): 157–97.

Fleming, P. and A. Spicer (2007) *Contesting the Corporation: Power, Resistance and Struggle in Organizations*. Cambridge: Cambridge University Press.

Fletcher, D.E. (2003) 'Framing organisational emergence: Discourse, identity and relationship', in C. Steyaert and D. Hjorth (eds), *New Movements in Entrepreneurship*. Cheltenham, UK and Northampton, MA, USA: Edward Elgar.

Fligstein, M. (1997) 'Social skill and institutional theory', *American Behavioural Scientist*, 40(4): 397–405.

Florida, R. (2004) *The Rise of the Creative Class*. London: Basic Books.

Foss, L. (2004) '"Going against the grain . . .": Construction of entrepreneurial identities through narratives' in D. Hjorth and C. Steyaert (eds), *Narrative and Discursive Approaches in Entrepreneurship*. Cheltenham, UK and Northampton, MA , USA: Edward Elgar.

Foucault, M. (1970) *The Order of Things*. London: Routledge.

Foucault, M. (1972) *The Archaeology of Knowledge*, trans. A. Sheridan Smith. London: Routledge.

Foucault, M. (1973) *The Birth of the Clinic*, trans. A. Sheridan Smith. London: Vintage.

Foucault, M. (1977) *Discipline and Punish: The Birth of the Prison*, trans. A. Sheridan Smith. London: Penguin.

Foucault, M. (1978) *The History of Sexuality, Volume 1: An Introduction*, trans. R. Hurley. London: Penguin.

Foucault, M. (1996) 'Sade: Sargent of sex' in S. Lotringer (ed.), *Foucault Live*, trans. L. Hochroth and J. Johnston. New York: Semiotext(e).

Foucault, M. (2003) *Abnormal: Lectures at the Collège de France, 1974–1975*, trans. G. Burchell. London: Verso.

Foucault, M. (2005) *History of Madness*, trans. J. Murphy. Oxford: Routledge.

Fournier, V. (1998) 'Stories of development and exploitation: Militant voices in an enterprise culture', *Organization*, 5(1): 55–80.

Fournier, V. and C. Grey (1999) 'Too much, too little and too often: A critique of du Gay's analysis of enterprise', *Organization*, 6(1): 107–28.

Frappier-Mazur, L. (1996) *Writing the Orgy: Power and Parody in Sade*, trans. G.C. Gill. Philadelphia, PA: Penn Press.

Frappier-Mazur, L. (1998) 'Sadean libertinage and the esthetics of violence', *Yale French Studies*, 94: 184–98.

Fraser, N. (1997) *Justice Interruptus: Critical Reflections on the 'Postsocialist' Condition*. New York: Routledge.

Fraser, N. and A. Honneth (2003) *Redistribution or Recognition: A Political-Philosophical Exchange*. London: Verso.

Freud, Sigmund (1938) 'Three contributions to the theory of sex' in *The Basic Writings of Sigmund Freud*, trans. A. Brill. New York: Modern Library.

Freud, Sigmund (1979) 'My views on the part played by sexuality in the aetiology of the neuroses' in *On Psychopathology*, trans. James Strachey. Pelican Freud Library vol. 10. London: Penguin.

Gabriel, Y. (1999) 'Beyond happy families: A critical reevaluation of the control-resistance-identity triangle', *Human Relations*, 52(2): 179–203.

Gartner, W.B. (1989) '"Who is an entrepreneur?" is the wrong question' *Entrepreneurship Theory and Practice*, (Summer): 47–68.

Gartner, W.B. (1990) 'What are we talking about when we talk about entrepreneurship?', *Journal of Business Venturing*, 5(1): 15–38.

Gartner, W.B. (1993) 'Words lead to deeds: Towards an organization emergence vocabulary', *Journal of Business Venturing*, 8(3): 231–40.

Garud, R., S. Jain and A. Kumaraswamy (2002) 'Institutional entrepreneurship in the sponsorship of common technological standards: The case of Sun Microsystems and Java', *Academy of Management Journal* 45(1): 196–214.

Goetz, S.J. and D. Freshwater (2001) 'State-level determinants of entrepreneurship and a preliminary measure of entrepreneurial climate', *Economic Development Quarterly*, 15(1): 58–70.

Grey, C. (1998) *Enterprise and Culture*. London: Routledge.

Grey, C. and H. Willmott (eds) (2005) *Critical Management Studies: A Reader*. Oxford: Oxford University Press.

Grosz, E. (1990) *Jacques Lacan: A Feminist Introduction*. London: Routledge.

Guardian (2004) 'The work is very hard. I'm depressed. I want to quit, but I have no freedom, no choice because I'm illegal', *Guardian*, 20 February, G2, p. 2.

Habermas, J. (1972) *Knowledge and Human Interests*, trans. J.J. Shapiro. London: Heinemann.

Habermas, J. (1984) *The Theory of Communicative Action, Volume 1: Reason and the Rationalization of Society*, trans. T. McCarthy. Oxford: Polity.

Habermas, J. (1987) *The Theory of Communicative Action, Volume 2: The Critique of Functionalist Reason*, trans. T. McCarthy. Oxford: Polity.

Hancock, P. and M. Tyler (2001) 'Managing subjectivity and the dialectic of self-consciousness: Hegel and organization theory', *Organization*, 8(4): 565–86.

Hardt, M. and A. Negri (1994) *Labor of Dionysus: A Critique of the State-Form*. Minneapolis: University of Minnesota Press.

Hardt, M. and A. Negri (2000) *Empire*. Cambridge, MA: Harvard University Press.

Hardy, C. and S. Maguire (2008) 'Institutional entrepreneurship' in R. Greenwood, C. Oliver, K. Sahlin and R. Suddaby (eds), *Sage Handbook of Organizational Institutionalism*. London: Sage.

Harvey, Oliver (2004) 'Slaves of King's Lynn', *Sun*, 14 February.

Heelas, P. and P. Morris (1992) *The Values of Enterprise Culture: A Moral Debate*. London: Routledge.

Hegel, G.W.F. (1977) *The Phenomenology of Spirit*, trans. A.V. Miller. Oxford: Oxford University Press.

Heidegger, Martin (2002) *The Essence of Truth*, trans. T. Sadler. London: Continuum.

Herron, L. and R.B. Robinson (1993) 'A structural model of the effect of entrepreneurial characteristics on venture performance', *Journal of Business Venturing*, 8(3): 281–94.

Hjorth, D. (2003) *Rewriting Entrepreneurship: For a New Perspective on Organisational Creativity*. Lund: Liber, Abstrakt and Copenhagen Business School Press.

Hjorth, D. (2005) 'Organizational entrepreneurship: With de Certeau on creating heterotopias (or spaces for play)', *Journal of Management Inquiry*, 14(4): 386–98.

Hjorth, D. and C. Steyaert (eds) (2004) *Narrative and Discursive Approaches in Entrepreneurship*. Cheltenham, UK and Northampton, MA, USA: Edward Elgar.

Hjorth, D. and C. Steyaert (2009a) 'Moving entrepreneurship: An incipiency' in Daniel Hjorth and Chris Steyaert (eds) *The Politics and Aesthetics of Entrepreneurship*. Cheltenham, UK and Northampton, MA, USA: Edward Elgar.

Hjorth, D. and C. Steyaert (eds) (2009b) *The Politics and Aesthetics of Entrepreneurship*. Cheltenham, UK and Northampton, MA, USA: Edward Elgar.

Hjorth, D., C. Jones and W.B. Gartner (2008) 'Recreating/recontextualising entrepreneurship', *Scandinavian Journal of Management*, 21: 81–4.

Hjorth, Daniel and Bengt Johannisson (forthcoming) 'Learning as an entrepreneurial process' in A. Fayolle (ed.), *Handbook of Research in Entrepreneurship Education*.

Johansson, A.W. (2004) 'Narrating the entrepreneur', *International Small Business Journal*, 22(3): 273–93.

Johnson, B.R. (1990) 'Towards a multi-dimensional model of entrepreneurship: The case of achievement motivation and the entrepreneur', *Entrepreneurship Theory and Practice*, 14(3): 39–54.

Jones, C. (2003) 'As if business ethics were possible, "within such limits". . .', *Organization*, 10(2): 223–48.

Jones, C. (2007) 'Read: Review of *Ecrits* by Jacques Lacan', *ephemera: theory and politics in organization*, 7(4): 615–21.

Kanter, R.M. (1990) *When Giants Learn to Dance*. New York: Free Press.

Kavanagh, T. (2006) 'Labour turns blind eye to the new slave trade', *Sun*, 27 March.

Keat, R. and N. Abercrombie (eds) (1991) *Enterprise Culture*. London: Routledge.

Keenan, T. (1998) 'Freedom, the law of another fable', *Yale French Studies*, 79: 231–51.

Kennedy, D., A. Norfolk and O. August (2004) 'Migrants at the mercy of gangs and the tides', *Times*, 7 February, p. 11.

Kets de Vries, M.F.R. (1985) 'The dark side of entrepreneurship', *Harvard Business Review*, 63(6): 160–67.

Kilby, P. (1971) *Entrepreneurship and Economic Development*. New York: Free Press.

Kirzner, I.M. (1973) *Competition and Entrepreneurship*. Chicago: University of Chicago Press.

Kirzner, I.M. (1997) 'Entrepreneurial discovery and competitive market forces: An Austrian approach', *Journal of Economic Literature*, 35: 60–85.

Klossowski, P. (1966) 'Nature as destructive principle' in A. Wainhouse and R. Seaver (eds), *The 120 Days of Sodom*. New York: Grove Press.

Knight, F. (1921/1939) *Risk, Uncertainty and Profit*. Boston: Houghton Mifflin.

Kristeva, J. (1984) *Powers of Horror: An Essay on Abjection*, trans. L.S. Roudiez. New York: Columbia University Press.

Lacan, J. (1979) *Seminar Eleven: The Four Fundamental Concepts of Psychoanalysis*, trans. A. Sheridan Smith. New York: Norton.

Lacan, J. (1988) *Seminar Two: The Ego in Freud's Theory and in the Technique of Psychoanalysis*, trans. J. Forester. Cambridge: Cambridge University Press.

Lacan, J. (2006a) *Ecrits*, trans. B. Fink. New York: Norton.

Lacan, J. (2006b) 'Kant with Sade' in *Ecrits*, trans. B. Fink. New York: Norton.

Laclau, E. (1996) 'Why do empty signifiers matter to politics?' in *Emancipation(s)*. London: Verso.

Laclau, E. and C. Mouffe (1985) *Hegemony and Socialist Strategy*. London: Verso.

Laporte, D. (2000) *History of Shit*, trans. R. El-Khoury and N. Benadid. Cambridge, MA: MIT Press.

Lawrence, F., H.-H. Pai, V. Dodd, H. Carer, D. Ward and J. Watts (2004) 'Victims of the sands and the snakeheads', *Guardian*, 7 February, p. 1.

Lee, D.Y. and E.W.K. Tsang (2001) 'The effects of entrepreneurial personality, background and network activity on venture growth', *Journal of Management Studies*, 38(4): 583–602.

Lefebvre, G. (1967) *The Coming of the French Revolution*. Princeton, NJ: Princeton University Press.

Levinas, E. (1989) 'Ethics as first philosophy' in S. Hand (ed.), *The Levinas Reader*. Oxford: Blackwell.

Levinas, E. (1999) 'The rights of the other man' in *Alterity and Transcendence*, trans. M.B. Smith. New York: Columbia University Press.

Levinas, E. (2006) *Humanism of the Other*, trans. N. Poller. Chicago: University of Illinois Press.

Lippert, O. and M. Walker (1997) *The Underground Economy: Global Evidence of Its Size and Impact*. University of British Columbia: The Fraser Institute.

Longenecker, J.G., J.A. McKinney and C.W. Moore (1988) 'Egoism and independence: Entrepreneurial ethics', *Organizational Dynamics*, 16: 64–72.

Longenecker, J.G., J.A. McKinney and C.W. Moore (1989a) 'Do smaller firms have higher ethics?', *Business and Society Review*, 71: 19–21.

Longenecker, J.G., J.A. McKinney and C.W. Moore: (1989b) 'Ethics in small business', *Journal of Small Business Management*, 27: 27–31.

Mandarini, M. (2005) 'Antagonism, contradiction, time: Conflict and organization in Antonio Negri' in C. Jones and R. Munro (eds), *Contemporary Organization Theory*. Oxford: Blackwell.

Manigrat, S. (1994) 'The founding rate of venture capital firms in 3 european countries (1970–1990)', *Journal of Business Venturing*, 9(6): 525–41.

Marcuse, H. (1964) *One Dimensional Man*. London: Abacus.

Marshall, A. (1890/1947) *Principles of Economics: An Introductory Volume* (8th edition). London: Macmillan.

Marx, K. (1894/1974) *Capital: A Critique of Political Economy, Volume 3*. London: Lawrence and Wishart.

Marx, K. (1954) *Capital: A Critique of Political Economy, Vol. 1.*, trans. S. Moore and E. Aveling. London: Lawrence and Wishart.

Marx, K. (1973) *Grundrisse: Foundations of the Critique of Political Economy (Rough Draft)*, trans. M. Nicolaus. London: Penguin.

Mauss, M. (1950) *The Gift: The Form and Reason for Exchange in Archaic Societies*, trans. W.D. Hall. London: Routledge.

McClelland, D. (1961) *The Achieving Society*, Princeton, NJ: Van Nostrand.

McTague, J. (2005) 'Going underground: America's shadow economy', *Barons*, 6 January.

Mennell, S. (1985) *All Manner of Food: Eating and Taste in England and France from the Middle Ages to the Present*. Oxford: Blackwell.

Mezias S.J. and J.C. Kuperman (2001) 'The community dynamics of entrepreneurship: The birth of the American film industry, 1895–1929', *Journal of Business Venturing*, 16(3): 209–33.

Mill, J.S. (1848/1898) *Principles of Political Economy*. London: Longmans.

Miller, J.-A. (1977) 'Translator's note' in Jacques Lacan *Ecrits*, trans. A. Sheridan Smith. New York: Norton.

Miller, J.-A. (1978) 'Suture (elements of the logic of the signifier)', *Screen*, 18(4): 24–34.

Milne, A.A. (1926) *Winnie-the-Pooh*. London: Methuen.

Milne, A.A. (1928) *The House at Pooh Corner*. London: Methuen.

Minniti, M. and W. Bygrave (1999) 'The microfoundations of entrepreneurship', *Entrepreneurship Theory and Practice*, 23(4): 41–52.

Morris, M.H., M. Schindehutte, J. Walton and J. Allen (2002) 'The ethical context of entrepreneurship: Proposing and testing a developmental framework', *Journal of Business Ethics*, 40(4): 331–61.

Mueller, S.L. and A.S. Thomas (2001) 'Culture and entrepreneurial potential: A nine country study of locus of control and innovativeness', *Journal of Business Venturing*, 16(1): 51–75.

Mun, T. (1664/1987) *England's Treasure by Forraign Trade, or, the Ballance of Our Forraign Trade Is the Rule of Our Treasures*. London: Thomas Clark.

Murtola, A.-M. (2008) 'Redeeming entrepreneurship', *Scandinavian Journal of Management*, 24: 127–9.

National Centre for Policy Analysis (1998) *The Underground Economy: Briefing Analysis 273*. Washington, DC: National Centre for Policy Analysis.

Negri, A. (2004) *Negri on Negri*, trans. M.B. DeBevoise. New York: Routledge.

Negri, A. (2008) *The Porcelain Workshop: For a New Grammar of Politics*, trans. N. Wedell. New York: Semiotext(e).

Newton, T. (1998) 'Theorizing subjectivity in organizations: The failure of Foucauldian studies?', *Organization Studies*, 19(3): 415–47.

Nicholson, A. (2004) 'Like Turner's slaves, the Chinese cocklers were the market's innocent victims', *Daily Telegraph*, 7 February.

Nicholson, L. and A.R. Anderson (2005) 'News and nuances of the entrepreneurial myth and metaphor: Linguistic games in entrepreneurial sense-making and sense-giving', *Entrepreneurship: Theory and Practice*, 29(2): 153–72.

Nietzsche, F. (1956) *The Genealogy of Morals*, trans. F. Golffing. New York: Doubleday.

Nietzsche, F. (1968) *The Will to Power*, trans. W. Kaufman and R.J. Hollingdale. New York: Vintage.

128 *Unmasking the entrepreneur*

Ogbor, J.O. (2000) 'Mythicizing and reification in entrepreneurial discourse: Ideology-critique of entrepreneurial studies', *Journal of Management Studies*, 37(5): 605–35.

Organization (forthcoming) Special issue on Jacques Lacan and Organization Studies.

Osborne, D. and T. Gaebler (1992) *Reinventing Government: How the Entrepreneurial Spirit Is Transforming the Public Sector*. New York: Plume.

Osbourne, Thomas R. (1983) *A Grande-Ecole for Grandes-Corps: The Recruitment and Training of the French Administrative Elite in the Nineteenth Century*. New York: Columbia University Press.

Pai, H.H. (2004) 'Fearful isolation, little hope, and even less cash', *Guardian*, 14 February, p. 7.

Parker, I. (1992) *Discourse Dynamics: Critical Analysis for Social and Individual Psychology*. London: Routledge.

Pêcheux, M. (1994) 'The mechanism of ideological (mis)recognition' in S. Žižek (ed.), *Mapping Ideology*. London: Verso.

Perren, L. and P.L. Jennings (2005) 'Government discourses on entrepreneurship: Issues of legitimization, subjugation, and power', *Entrepreneurship Theory and Practice*, 29(2): 173–84.

Petty, W. (1662/1997) 'A treatise on taxes and contributions' in C.H. Hull (ed.), *The Economic Writings of Sir William Petty, Volume 1*. London: Routledge.

Pfeffer, J. (2003) 'Economic logic and language in organization studies: Undermining critical thinking'. Paper presented to the 63rd Annual Meeting of the Academy of Management, Seattle, August.

Phillips, N., T.B. Lawrence, and C. Hardy (2004) 'Discourse and institutions', *Academy of Management Review*, 29(4): 635–52.

Pitt, M. (1998) 'A tale of two gladiators: "Reading" entrepreneurs as texts', *Organization Studies*, 19(3): 387–414.

Polanyi, K. (1945) *The Great Transformation*. Boston: Beacon.

Quesnay, F. (1759/1972) *Tableau économique*, ed. M. Kuczinski and R. Meek. London: Macmillan.

Radaev, V. (1993) 'Emerging Russian entrepreneurship as viewed by the experts', *Economic and Industrial Democracy*, 14 (Supplement): 55–77.

Rae, D. (2004) 'Practical theories from entrepreneurs' stories: Discursive approaches to entrepreneurial learning', *Journal of Small Business and Enterprise Development*, 11(2): 195–202.

Reed, M. (1998) 'Organizational analysis as discourse analysis: A critique' in D. Grant, C. Oswick and T. Keenoy (eds), *Discourse and Organization*. London: Sage.

Reed, M. (2000) 'The limits of discourse analysis in organizational analysis', *Organization*, 7(3): 524–30.

Reed, M. (2009) 'Critical realism in critical management studies' in M. Alvesson, T. Bridgman and H. Willmott (eds.), *The Oxford Handbook of Critical Management Studies*. Oxford: Oxford University Press.

Rehn, A. (2004) *The Serious Unreal: Notes on Business and Frivolity*. Åbo: Dvalin.

Rehn, A. (2008) 'On meta-theory and moralization: A prolegomena to a critique of management studies', *Organization*, 15(4): 598–609.

Rehn, A. and S. Taalas (2004a) 'Crime and assumptions in entrepreneurship' in D. Hjorth and C. Steyaert (eds) *Narrative and Discursive Approaches in Entrepreneurship*. Cheltenham, UK and Northampton, MA, USA: Edward Elgar.

Rehn, A. and S. Taalas (2004b) '"Znakomstva i svyazi" (acquaintances and connections): *Blat*, the Soviet Union, and mundane entrepreneurship', *Entrepreneurship and Regional Development*, 16(May): 235–50.

Ricardo, D. (1817/1973) *The Principles of Political Economy and Taxation*. London: Dent.

Ritter, A. (1998) 'Entrepreneurship, microenterprise, and public policy in Cuba: Promotion, containment, or asphyxiation?', *Journal of Inter-American Studies and World Affairs*, 40(2): 63–94.

Roberts, J. (2005) 'The power of the "imaginary" in disciplinary processes' *Organization*, 12(5): 619–42.

Rose, N. (1996) 'The death of the social? Refiguring the territory of government', *Economy and Society*, 25(3): 327–56.

Ruef, M. and M. Lounsbury (eds) (2007) *The Sociology of Entrepreneurship* (Research in the Sociology of Organizations, Volume 25). Oxford: Elsevier.

Salecl, R. (1998) *(Per)versions of Love and Hate*. New York: Verso.

Sarason, Y., T. Dean and J.F. Dillard (2006) 'Entrepreneurship as a nexus of individual and opportunity: A structuration view', *Journal of Business Venturing*, 21: 286–305.

Say, J.-B. ([1803] 1821/1964) *A Treatise on Political Economy, or, the Production, Distribution and Consumption of Wealth*, trans. C.R. Princep. New York: Augustus Kelley.

Schlosser, E. (2003) *Reefer Madness and Other Tales of the American Underground*. London: Penguin.

Schmitt, C. (1985) *Political Theology: Four Chapters on the Concept of Sovereignty*, trans. G. Schwab. Chicago: University of Chicago Press.

Schmitt, C. (1996) *The Concept of the Political*, trans. G. Schwab. Chicago: University of Chicago Press.

Schneider, M. and P. Teske (1992) 'Towards a theory of the political entrepreneur: Evidence from local government', *American Political Science Review*, 86(3): 737–47.

Schrift, A. (ed.) (1997) *The Logic of the Gift: Toward an Ethic of Generosity*. London: Routledge.

Schumpeter, J. (1934) *The Theory of Economic Development*. New York: Oxford University Press.

Schumpeter, J. (1944) *Capitalism, Socialism and Democracy*. London: Allen and Unwin.

Scott, W.G. (1974) 'Organization theory: A reassessment', *Academy of Management Journal*, 17(2): 242–54.

Scott, W.R. (1999) *Institutions and Organizations*. London: Sage.

Shane, S. (2000) 'Prior knowledge and the discovery of entrepreneurial opportunities', *Organization Science*, 11(4): 448–69.

Shane S. (2003) *A General Theory of Entrepreneurship: The Individual-Opportunity Nexus*. Cheltenham, UK and Northampton, MA, USA: Edward Elgar.

Shane, S. and S. Venkataraman (2000) 'The promise of entrepreneurship as a field of research', *Academy of Management Review*, 25(1): 217–26.

Shapiro, Michael (1993) *Reading 'Adam Smith': Desire, History and Value*. London: Sage.

Shaver, K.G. and L.R. Scott (1991) 'Person, process, choice: The psychology of new venture creation', *Entrepreneurship Theory and Practice*, 16(2): 23–45.

Sköld, D. and A. Rehn (2007) 'Makin' it, by keeping it real: Street talk, rap music and the forgotten entrepreneurship from "the 'hood"', *Group & Organization Management*, 32(1): 50–78.

Smilor, R.W. and H.R. Feeser (1991) 'Chaos and the entrepreneurial process: Patterns and policy implications for technology entrepreneurship', *Journal of Business Venturing*, 6(3): 165–72.

Smith, B. (1988) *Contingencies of Value: Alternative Perspectives for Critical Theory*. Cambridge, MA: Harvard University Press.

Soldatenko, M.A. (1999) 'Made in the USA: Latinas/os?, garment work, and ethnic conflict in Los Angeles' sweat shops', *Cultural Studies*, 13(2): 319–34.

Solymossy, E. and J.K. Masters (2002) 'Ethics through an entrepreneurial lens: Theory and observation', *Journal of Business Ethics*, 28(3): 227–41.

Sommer, S.M. and D.H.B. Welsh (2000) 'The ethical orientation of Russian entrepreneurs', *Applied Psychology: An International Review*, 49(4): 688–708.

Sørensen, B.M. (2005) 'Immaculate defecation: On the organization theory of Deleuze and Guattari' in Campbell Jones and Rolland Munro (eds), *Contemporary Organization Theory*. Oxford: Blackwell.

Sørensen, B.M. (2008) '"Behold, I am making all things new": The entrepreneur as savior in the age of creativity', *Scandinavian Journal of Management*, 24: 85–93.

Sørensen, B.M. (2009) 'The entrepreneurial utopia: Miss Black Rose and the holy communion' in D. Hjorth and C. Steyaert (eds) *The Politics and Aesthetics of Entrepreneurship*. Cheltenham, UK and Northampton, MA, USA: Edward Elgar.

Spencer, R. (2004) 'EU states agree to let in Chinese on tourist visas', *Daily Telegraph*, 13 February, p. 7.

Spicer, A. and P. Fleming (2007) 'Intervening in the inevitable: Contesting globalization in a public organization', *Organization*, 14(4): 517–41.

Spivak, G.C. (1996) 'Scattered speculations on the question of value' in D. Landry and G. MacLean (eds), *The Spivak Reader*. London: Routledge.

Stablein, R. and W. Nord (1985) 'Practical and emancipatory interest in organizational symbolism: A review and evaluation', *Journal of Management*, 11(2): 13–28.

Starr, J.A. and I.C. MacMillan (1990) 'Resource cooptation via social contracting: Resource acquisition strategies for new ventures', *Strategic Management Journal*, 11: 79–92.

Stavrakakis, Y. (2008) 'Subjectivity and the organized other: Between symbolic authority and fantasmic enjoyment', *Organization Studies*, 29(7): 1037–59.

Steyaert, C. and D. Hjorth (eds) (2003) *New Movements in Entrepreneurship*. Cheltenham, UK and Northampton, MA, USA: Edward Elgar.

Steyaert, C. and D. Hjorth (eds) (2006) *Entrepreneurship as Social Change*. Cheltenham, UK and Northampton, MA, USA: Edward Elgar.

Stubbs, J. (2005) 'Sade' in C. Jones and D. O'Doherty (eds), *Manifestos for the Business School of Tomorrow*. Åbo: Dvalin.

Sun (2004) 'Grim "slave" life', *Sun*, 7 February.

Swedberg, R. (ed.) (2000) *Entrepreneurship: The Social Science View*. Oxford: Oxford University Press.

Tarrow, S. (1998) *Power in Movement: Social Movements, Collective Action and Politics*. Cambridge, MA: Cambridge University Press.

Teal, E.J. and A.B. Carroll (1999) 'Moral reasoning skills: Are entrepreneurs different?', *Journal of Business Ethics*, 19(3): 229–40.

ten Bos, R. (2006) 'The new severity: On managerial masochism'. Paper presented at the Asia-Pacific Researchers in Organization Studies Conference, Melbourne, 4–7 December.

Thomas, A.S. and S.L. Mueller (2000) 'A case for comparative entrepreneurship: Assessing the relevance of culture', *Journal of International
Business Studies*, 31(2): 287–301.

Thompson, P. and S. Ackroyd (1995). 'All quiet on the workplace front?:
A critique of recent trends in British industrial sociology', *Sociology*,
29(4): 615–33.

Thomson, A. (2004) 'Give Chinese cockle-pickers a chance', *Daily
Telegraph*, 13 February, p. 26.

Thornton, P.H. (1999) 'The sociology of entrepreneurship', *Annual Review
of Entrepreneurship*, 25: 19–46.

Tilly, Charles (1986) *The Contentious French*. Cambridge, MA: Cambridge
University Press.

Toynbee, Polly (2003) *Hard Work: Life in Low-Pay Britain*. London:
Bloomsbury.

Tozer, J. (2004) 'Death toll in cockle tragedy reaches 20', *Daily Telegraph*,
16 February, p. 6.

Turgot, A.R.J. (1774/1999) *Reflections on the Formation and Distribution
of Wealth*, trans. Keneth Jupp. London: Othila.

US Department of Labor (1992) *The Underground Economy in the United
States: Occassional Papers on the Informal Sector, 2*. Washington, DC:
US Government Printing Office.

van Praag, C.M. and J.S. Cramer (2001) 'The roots of entrepreneurship and labour demand: Individual ability and low risk aversion',
Economica, 68(269): 45–62.

Vanheule, S., A. Lievrouw and P. Verhaeghe (2003) 'Burnout and inter-
subjectivity: A psychoanalytical study from a Lacanian perspective',
Human Relations, 56(3): 321–38.

Veblen, T. (1899) *The Theory of the Leisure Class: An Economic Study of
Institutions*. London: Unwin.

Velamuri, S.R. (2002) 'Entrepreneurship, altruism and the good society',
Ruffin Series in Business Ethics, 3: 125–42.

Venkatesh, S.A. (2006) *Off the Books: The Underground Economy of the
Urban Poor*. Cambridge, MA: Harvard University Press.

Virno, P. (2008) *Multitude: Between Innovation and Negation*, trans. I.
Bertoletti, J. Cascaito and A. Casson. New York: Semiotext(e).

Volkov, V. (2002) *Violent Entrepreneurs: The Use of Force in the Making
of Russian Capitalism*. Ithaca, NY: Cornell University Press.

Ward, D. and J. Watts (2004) 'Morecambe cockle pickers return to work',
Guardian, 11 February.

Watts, J. (2004) 'Cockler deaths: "Our life is bloody hard here"', *Guardian*,
9 February, p. 4.

Weick, Karl (1995) *Sensemaking in Organizations*. London: Sage.

Weick, Karl (2001) *Making Sense of the Organization*. Oxford: Blackwell.

Westall, A., P. Ramsden and J. Foley (2000) *Micro-Entrepreneurs: Creating Enterprising Communities*. London: New Economics Foundation.

Williams, C. (2006) *The Hidden Enterprise Culture: Entrepreneurship in the Underground Economy*. Cheltenham, UK and Northampton, MA, USA: Edward Elgar.

Woodley, T. (2004) 'The underbelly of globalisation: The Chinese workers who died were victims of cowboy capitalism', *Guardian*, 7 February, p. 22.

Wu, C.F. (2002) 'The relationship of ethical decision-making to business ethics and performance in Taiwan', *Journal of Business Ethics*, 25(3): 162–76.

Wyschogrod, E., J.-J. Goux and E. Boynton (eds) (2002) *The Enigma of Gift and Sacrifice*. New York: Fordham University Press.

Yurtsever, G. (2003) 'Measuring the moral entrepreneurial personality', *Social Behavior and Personality*, 31(1): 1–12.

Žižek, S. (1989) *The Sublime Object of Ideology*. London: Verso.

Žižek, S. (1997) *The Plague of Fantasies*. London: Verso.

Žižek, S. (1999) *The Ticklish Subject: The Absent Centre of Political Ontology*. London: Verso.

Žižek, S., E.L. Santner and K. Reinhard (2006) *The Neighbor: Three Inquiries in Political Theology*. Chicago: University of Chicago Press.

Index